Letting God Create Your Day

Volume 7

Paul A. Bartz

Creation Moments

The Scripture quotations in this publication are from **The Holy Bible, King James Version,** World Publishing Company.

Letting God Create Your Day: Volume 7
By Paul A. Bartz

Creation Moments, Inc.
P.O. Box 839 Foley, Minnesota 56329
www.creationmoments.com
800-422-4253

ISBN 1-882510-20-8

Printed in the United States of America
Printing and production costs for this book were underwritten by supporters of Creation Moments.

Foreword

It is with a mixture of excitement and sadness that I write this Foreword to the seventh volume of *Letting God Create Your Day*. Author Paul A. Bartz would have written it himself if his Savior hadn't taken him to his eternal home to attend to more important business.

Before cancer took his life in 2013, Paul wrote the scripts for the Creation Moments broadcast ever since it first took to the airwaves in 1986. In fact, Paul wrote all of the scripts for the program that have since been collected into six volumes of *Letting God Create Your Day* – one for each day of Creation. Now, with the release of the seventh volume, Paul's earthly labors for the Lord have ceased. He leaves behind a body of work that has blessed and continues to be a blessing to countless millions all over the world.

Though Paul didn't have a formal science education, he was delighted by every branch of science and was able to readily comprehend a diverse range of scientific subjects that would leave most people in the dark. As a pastor and teacher of God's inerrant Word, he also possessed a thorough understanding of Scripture, and he well knew the monumental harm caused by the lie of godless evolution.

Not only was Paul a voracious reader of science books and magazines, he was gifted at picking out science stories in the news and retelling them in a way that brought Christians to their knees in worship. He had a knack for taking complex scientific subjects and making them understandable to readers of all ages. And he ended almost all of his scripts with biblical insights that came from a pastor's heart.

I never met Paul in person, but I do have a personal story to tell. Like other Christians, I have often experienced times when God seemed distant. Such dark times drew me closer to God's Word, especially the Psalms, which told me that "God is our refuge and strength, a very present help in trouble" (Psalm 46:1). But I also found encouragement in the pages of the previous volumes of *Letting God Create Your Day*. As Paul Bartz made so clear in many of his scripts, if God cared so greatly about even the lowliest of His creatures, surely He cared for me, His child.

Now that Creation Moments has asked me to continue the work that Paul Bartz started so many years ago, I pick up his mantle with a great deal of trepidation. Who can hope to follow in such a person's footsteps? Nevertheless, I pray that the Lord will guide me in this work just as He guided Pastor Bartz.

I can't think of a better way to bring this Foreword to a close than by repeating what Paul wrote at the end of his Foreword to the first volume of *Letting God Create Your Day*. I believe these words best sum up what he was thinking while writing more than 1,600 Creation Moments radio scripts:

It is my prayer that this edition of Letting God Create Your Day *will edify you and draw you closer to our Creator and His saving grace to you in our Lord Jesus Christ.*

Steve Schwartz
Creation Moments Writer/Editor

Gossiping Plants

Isaiah 40:8

"The grass withereth, the flower fadeth: but the word of our God shall stand for ever."

The venus flytrap senses a fly and, in less than a second, its trap springs shut. It will eat today. A new area of science is plant behavior. Plant behaviorists point out that plants, like the venus flytrap that interact with animals, have to move on an animal scale. We have traditionally thought of plants as inactive living things that just sit there. But as we learn more about them, we are beginning to discover that plants are much more active than we ever thought.

Other plants move as well, often when they interact with animals. But sometimes not. When a white mulberry tree opens its blooms, they open at half the speed of sound. But there's more than this to plant behavior. Scientists have learned that plants have memory, despite the lack of a nervous system or brain. Yet, when a leaf has mobilized its defenses against a predator in the past, it will do so more quickly the next time the threat returns. Previously we have talked about how plants communicate by emitting scents. When a leaf is attacked, a scent is emitted, warning surrounding leaves and plants. Scientists now call this "plant gossiping."

When we see how much ability God has given even plants, we are led to realize, thankfully, that God has been even more generous to us.

Prayer: Father, I rejoice and thank You for Your generous gifts to me, most especially for Your grace and forgiveness. Amen.

Ref: *Science News*, 6/20/09, pp. 16-19, Susan Milius, "No brainer behavior."

Did Noah's Flood Affect Mars, Too?

Genesis 7:11

"In the six hundredth year of Noah's life ... were all the fountains of the great deep broken up, and the windows of heaven were opened."

One of the biggest headlines in planetary exploration in recent years was the confirmation that at one time Mars had water. Further exploration and study reveals evidence that there was once quite a lot of moving water on the surface of Mars.

With two rovers having sent back pictures and information from the surface, plus an orbiter exploring the surface, evidence of water action began to mount. At first, small features that looked like they were formed by moving water were discovered. Soon, it looked like that there was widespread water action in the southern hemisphere. Besides erosion, there is widespread evidence of the type of rocks that form underwater. Now, similar evidence suggests widespread water action in the northern lowlands as well. One of the most dramatic features could be the Mars version of the Grand Canyon. Called Valles Marineris, it is 2,000 miles long, 400 miles wide and five miles deep. It is so big, it can be seen from Earth with a good telescope. It would take catastrophic amounts of water to form such a canyon.

While the Bible doesn't say anything about the flood that would suggest Mars was involved, some creation geologists say that it may have been. Once thing is certain. This water action did not take place billions of years ago as those who believe in evolution say.

Prayer: Lord, I thank You for Your trustworthy Word which judges sin and speaks the welcome words of the Gospel to us. Amen.

Ref: *Acts & Facts*, 9/10, pp. 12-13, Larry Vardiman, "News From the Red Planet."

An Elegant Quilt of Relationships

Psalm 104:16-17

"The trees of the LORD are full of sap; the cedars of Lebanon, which he hath planted; Where the birds make their nests: as for the stork, the fir trees are her house."

There are many incredible designs around us that are unlikely to exist if everything is the result of mindless chance. Many birds eat insects through the summer. While such high protein diets like this are good in mating and reproductive season, they do not prepare the birds to survive the cold weather of winter.

What they need to do is build a layer of fat both for calorie storage as well as insulation. So, as winter nears, the berries that have been growing and ripening all summer on various shrubs become more numerous. The high sugar content of the berries' juice helps the birds to quickly build up fat. The freeze on cold fall mornings even helps to increase the sugar concentration in the berries. Even more amazing is that the various types of berries eaten by the birds ripen in a staggered fashion so that berry season is long and the supplies are always available. For example, as the elderberry supply is just about consumed, highbush cranberries are in production. Often, the summer's hatchlings' plumage doesn't reach full color until they eat the various pigments in the berries, and those pigments are incorporated into the new feathers. In exchange, the birds spread the seeds in the berries.

All of these complex, interrelated systems depend on each other in an elegant, fine-tuned design.

Prayer: Father, thank You for the beauty and song of the birds which bless and enrich our lives. Amen.

Ref: http://www.startribune.com/templates/Print_this_story?sid=64091192, 10/14/09, Val Cunningham, "Why bushes are better for birds."

The Ants' Road Department

Psalm 5:8

"Lead me, O LORD, in thy righteousness because of mine enemies; make thy way straight before my face."

You're driving down the road and all of a sudden traffic slows to a crawl. Finally, you get to the cause of the slowdown – a big pothole in the road that causes people to slow down and drive around.

Some ants have the same problem. A species of army ant found in Brazil sends out hunters every morning. They travel, several ants wide, looking for other ants – even things as large as scorpions – to attack and return to home base. However, paths in the Brazilian jungle can be rough and even have potholes. When the ants encounter an ant-sized pothole in their road, one choice might be to slow down and narrow their path to get around it. Researchers say that such slowdowns can cut the amount of food delivered home by thirty percent. So, instead, the first ant to encounter such a pothole measures it. If the hole is his size, he fills the pothole with his own body. If the pothole is small, a full grown ant will leave it for a smaller ant to fill.

While God gave these army ants this ability to efficiently overcome obstacles in their path, He has done far more for us. When Scripture talks about making our ways straight before the Lord, it is speaking of Christ's righteousness which is ours by grace through faith.

Prayer: Lord Jesus Christ, thank You for the gift of Your righteousness. Help me always treasure and live in this gift. Amen.

Ref: *Science News*, 6/2/07, pp. 340-341, S. Milius, "Pothole Pals."

What Amoebas Know

Psalm 119:105

"Thy word is a lamp unto my feet, and a light unto my path."

When lost in the forest with no clues to where to go, humans tend to go in circles. And we have brains. Amoebas, which don't have brains, somehow manage not to end up going in circles when they have no clues where to go.

Normally, amoebas look for food by picking up its scent. When amoebas detect something good to eat, they move in its direction by extending parts of its body called pseudopods. However, when there are no scents to follow, many single-celled creatures tend to wander aimlessly. This turns out to be a very inefficient strategy for finding food. That's because, just like humans, they end up wandering in circles. But after careful study, researchers from Princeton University have concluded that amoebas somehow manage to avoid this problem. Somehow, though they have no brain, they appear to remember where they have been. They suggest that forming pseudopods causes a type of temporary scarring on its cell wall which serves as a type of memory.

While amoebas are just looking for food, we ultimately seek an eternity with our Creator. Many people do not know of or do not believe God's Word and end up with lives that wander in spiritual circles. But God's Word brings heaven's light into our lives which lights the way to heaven through our Lord Jesus Christ.

Prayer: Father, thank You for the light of Your Word in this dark world. Help me to always walk in its light. Amen.

Ref: *Science News*, 3/31/07, p. 205, D.C., "How smart are amoebas?"

What Color Are Peacock Feathers?

Job 39:13

"Gavest thou the goodly wings unto the peacocks? or wings and feathers unto the ostrich?"

What color would you say that peacock feathers are? If you answered "black", you would be right. How can that be?

Those colors you think you see in the peacock's tail seem to be a very clever trick played on you by the wily peacock. Where do the colors come from? We have to go to the billionth-of-a-meter scale to answer that question. At that scale, you would see that every tiny branch of each feather is coated with a huge collection of rods. As the light bounces off of them, different wavelengths of light go in different directions. Some even set up interference patterns which cancel out certain wavelengths. The result is that the eye detects the vast array of colors that we associate with the peacock.

But there is more to the story. Obviously, the quality of the peacock's show depends on how the light strikes and reflects off the feathers. Scientists believe that's where the peacock's strutting, dancing backward and even tail rattling comes in. After studying several populations of peacocks, they have concluded that the peacock seeks to place himself between the sun and the peahen to give her the best show.

Incredible beauty remains in the creation since the fall. We can't imagine the unspeakable beauty that was originally placed into the creation by our wise Creator.

Prayer: Father, I thank You and marvel at the beauty that remains in the creation even after the fall. Amen.

Ref: http://www.sciencenews.org/view/feature/id/32451/title/How_they_shine, 6/7/08, Susan Milius, "How They Shine."

The Literal Beauty of the Trees' Immune System

Matthew 2:11

"And when they were come into the house ... they presented unto him gifts; gold, and frankincense and myrrh."

Many people are unaware that amber, often treated like a gemstone, is actually produced by trees. Many don't know that amber shows up at important points in Scripture.

Amber is not the hardened sap of a tree. Rather, it is part of a tree's immune system. When a tree trunk or branch is injured, the tree produces amber as a thick liquid which seals the wound and then hardens – sort of an instant bandage. Often, people associate amber with long ages, thinking that it takes millions of years to form amber. If that were the case, it wouldn't make a very good bandage. Many times, amber will contain surprisingly intact insect remains or even plant parts. If amber took long ages to form, any such plant or animal material would have decayed. Another indicator that amber is not millions of years old is that still-living bacteria and yeast cells have been found in amber.

Because amber needs to be tough to protect an injured tree, it lasts much longer than the tree needs it. That it is attractive makes it desired for jewelry. Some amber is quite aromatic when it is burned. Such amber is called myrrh in the Bible. And in some traditional cultures, amber is also used as medicine. Amber, with its many uses, is a blessing from our Creator.

Prayer: Lord Jesus, when You came among us, the Wise Men gave You myrrh, your blessing to us and the trees. Thank You. Amen.

Ref: *Acts & Facts*, 9/10, p. 17, Brian Thomas, "Amber Jewelry: A Conversation Piece for Creation Evidence."

The Spookfish's Spooky Eyes

1 Corinthians 13:12

"For now we see through a glass, darkly; but then face to face: now I know in part; but then shall I know even as also I am known."

Perhaps you have seen a reflecting telescope. It has a precision-designed concave mirror that collects the incoming light and focuses it on a magnifying lens where the image is seen. The mirror on the Hubble Space Telescope had a faulty mirror when it was launched that had to be corrected. Any effective vision system that includes a mirror to reflect light must focus very precisely.

While the spookfish has been known for 120 years, the first living specimen was only recently examined by science. It got its name because of its pale, ghostly appearance. At first, it looks like the spookfish, which lives thousands of feet below the surface of the water, has four eyes. However, its two eyes are actually split in two. Half of each eye looks up, watchful for both predators and food. The other half of each eye looks down. Any bioluminescence coming from below is reflected into this part of the eye by a concave mirror. This precise structure uses guanine crystals, which make scales shiny to reflect the light.

Given the precision required for clear vision when a mirror is involved, you cannot arrive at the spookfish's vision system through small, random changes. As Paul says, an imperfect mirror results in imperfect vision. The spookfish is an example of the irreducible complexity of so many of God's precision designs.

Prayer: Dear Father, give me clear spiritual vision so that I may see my life and Your will through the eyes of faith. Amen.

Ref: *Science Illustrated*, 10/09, p. 22, "Mirror Vision."

Did Some Fossilized Creatures Die of Fossilization?

Genesis 7:20

"Fifteen cubits upward did the waters prevail; and the mountains were covered."

Every science text explains how slow processes over long periods of time could result in the fossil beds we know today. However, fossil beds all over the world tell a very different story when they are allowed to tell their own story.

In many cases, it appears that burial and fossilization happened so rapidly that some scientists have suggested that some of these creatures died of fossilization. There are many interesting examples of fossilized crinoids. They were made up of soft tissue which held harder plates together. It takes only a number of days after death for the soft tissue to decay to the point that it can't hold harder plates together. But in the Niagara Gorge of New York, many intact crinoids may be found. Wyoming's Green River sedimentary rocks have multitudes of small, minnow-like fish that were preserved in great detail in the rocks. If their burial was not almost instantaneous, and fossilization did not take place in a matter of days, these fossils would not be there today. Fossil beds in Brazil preserve more than just fish. Tender tissue such as muscles, stomachs and even gills are preserved. What normally happens to such tissues when a fish dies calls for fossilization within five hours of death.

When read properly, the scientific evidence does not contradict God's story of history. In fact, it often confirms it.

Prayer: Father, the flood was Your judgment on sin. I thank You that You judged my sin when Jesus was on the cross. Amen.

Ref: *Acts & Facts*, 8/07, p. 14, William A. Hoesch, "Lagerstatten!"

A Walk on the Dark Side

Ecclesiastes 8:16-17b

"When I applied my heart to know wisdom and to see the business that is done on earth, even though one sees no sleep day or night, then I saw all the work of God, that a man cannot find out the work that is done under the sun."

A scientific mistake has led to several discoveries about bumblebees. As scientists closed up their lab for the night at the State University of New York at Stony Brook, one of them accidentally left on an infrared TV monitoring system. When the researchers returned the next morning, they discovered that the bumblebees they had been studying were slipping out of the nest in the dark for a midnight snack. No, they didn't fly. Instead, they walked to the food supply the scientists had provided. This led the scientists to further study how bees navigate in the dark. When researchers moved their feeder, the bees walked through the dark to its old location. When scientists changed the position of the floor on which the bees walked, they followed their old path, even though it went in the wrong direction. After scientists cleaned the surface on which the bees walked, the bees still went in the compass direction of the original position of their feeder. These results have led the scientists to believe that bumblebees navigate both by smell and by some sort of internal magnetic compass. Neither of these two facts was known before. One final discovery is that bee feeding has two peak times, midday and midnight. Clearly, there is a lot more to learn.

God's creativity in providing all His creatures with the abilities they need appears to be unlimited. No matter how sophisticated science becomes, it will never run out of things to learn about God's creativity. This is another evidence that we are not the product of chance evolution.

Prayer: We thank You, Father, for Your wonderful creativity in all things. Amen.

Ref: S.M. Night life discovered for bumblebees, *Science News*, v.155, p.78

Two Languages that May Support Biblical History

Genesis 11:7

"Come, let us go down and there confuse their language, that they may not understand one another's speech."

The Bible's account of human history leads to the conclusion that the languages of the world had their birth at the Tower of Babel about 4,300 years ago. Evolutionists, however, place the separation of a Siberian and native North American group at thousands of years before that. Yet one linguist has found remarkable similarities between these two language groups that suggest these groups separated from one another much more recently.

The usual evolutionary model has native North Americans crossing a land bridge from Siberia to populate North America at least 10,000 years ago. So, one linguistic researcher wondered if there were any Siberian Languages that were related to North American languages. He compared the Ket language with the Na-Dene family of languages. The Ket language is spoken only in central Siberia and appears to have no linguistic relatives. The Na-Dene family of languages is spoken in western Canada and Alaska. He found that the two languages have 36 protowords that sound the same and have the same or similar meanings in both languages. Among the similarities are terms for body parts, natural phenomena, (like snow and animals), and every day things. This evidence strongly suggests that the two languages are related; however, other linguists are not convinced.

If Ket and Na-Dene are truly related to each other, then surely these language groups separated more recently than the usual evolutionary model suggests. This conclusion would support a literal reading of the Biblical history.

Prayer: We thank You, Lord, that Your Word is trustworthy in all that it says. Amen.

Ref: B. Bower, Tongue ties across continents draw fire, *Science News*, November 14, 1998, v.154, p.311

Biblical "Kinds" Are Not Necessarily "Species"

Genesis 1:11

"Then God said, 'Let the earth bring forth grass, the herb that yields seed, and the fruit tree that yields fruit according to its kind, whose seed is in itself, on the earth'; and it was so."

Back in the 1970's, San Franciscans decided to restore their salt marshes. Cordgrass was among the plants that were being restored to the marshes. However, the cordgrass that was used in the restoration was a commercially available species from the eastern United States, not the California species. At the time, those working on the restoration did not realize that the two almost identical species have some important differences.

The eastern species, which is taller than the California species, produces 21 times as much pollen as the California cordgrass. The eastern species also produces eight times as many seeds as the California species. But the two species are similar enough to cross pollinate and produce a fertile hybrid with many of the eastern species' characteristics. Both the eastern species and the hybrid are able to colonize much closer to the water than the native California species.

This battle between the eastern and California cordgrass illustrates some Scriptural truths. First, the "kinds" that Scripture says everything is supposed to reproduce after are not the same as species. "Species" are a human designation while "kinds" are God's designation. These two species of cordgrass are obviously of the same kind since they produce fertile hybrids. And since the eastern species is more robust than the California species, it could well be closer to the original kind that God created.

Prayer: Father, I pray that I may truly have the characteristics of Your child through Jesus Christ, my Lord. Amen.

Ref: S. Milius, Superstud grass menaces San Francisco Bay, *Science News*, November 14, 1998, v.154, p. 310

When Is a Billion Years Not a Billion Years?

Genesis 5:5

"So all the days that Adam lived were nine hundred and thirty years; and he died."

We often hear evolutionary scientists talking about this or that fossil that is, they say, "millions" or "billions" of years old. On the other hand, the Bible preserves ancient calendars from the time of Adam, such as in Genesis 5, which allow us to place the creation at only a few thousand years ago. How do evolutionists arrive at those millions of years?

All dating systems in use are based on the supposed evolutionary progression of life. Some people think that there are radioactive dating methods that are independent of the evolutionary tree, but the technical literature admits that this is not the case. Rock samples are dated by what are called index fossils. If a given rock sample has a certain shell in it, and the evolutionary tree says that creature lived 55 million years ago, the rock is dated at 55 million evolutionary years. That this system doesn't always work the way evolutionists expect was illustrated by a rock that was recently discovered in India. The rock sample, from a layer previously dated from other samples, was said to be 1.1 billion years old. Yet it had worm burrows in it. Evolutionist history says that worms didn't evolve until half a billion years ago. Another evolutionist examined the rock and said he found shells in it that date it at 545 million years ago. Yet other scientists looked at the rock and said that the shells weren't really shells. So they are now stuck with dates that conflict with each other by more that 100 percent. Rocks will continue to be found which don't fit into the evolutionary time table because they, and all life, were formed by God not millions but only thousands of years ago.

Prayer: I thank You, Father, that You have made everything and told us about it in Your perfect Word. In Jesus' Name. Amen.

Ref: R.M. A rock that lies about its age, *Science News,* November 21, 1998, v. 154, p.332

Two Pairs of Ears Offer a Telling Story

Psalm 78:1

"Give ear, O my people, to my law; incline your ears to the words of my mouth."

Did you ever wonder what those folds in your ear do? Scientists have recently confirmed their suspicions that those little folds, called pinnae, help you tell where sounds are coming from. All those little folds amplify or weaken certain frequencies, and your brain processes these changes and figures out where the sound you hear is coming from.

Now comes the mystery. Your pinnae are unique to you. Pinnae have been compared to finger prints—each person has unique pinnea. This means that your pinnae do different things to the sounds you hear than, say, what your wife hears. Yet, if we both hear the same sound, we can both tell where it is coming from. Scientists have theorized that the brain is designed to learn the unique shape of its pinnae, and from that, to learn how to tell the source of a sound. That theory was recently confirmed. Scientists gave volunteers plastic molds designed to change the shape of their pinnae. After the molds were implanted into their ears, the subjects discovered that it took several weeks for them to develop the ability to discern the height of a source of sound. Even more interesting is that when the molds were removed, the subjects' did not have to relearn how to tell the height of a sound. One researcher compared this to learning a new language. The brains were now able to effectively use two different sets of pinnae.

This ability to relearn how to tell the height and direction of sound, even if our pinnae are injured, points to a wise Creator Who provides for our needs. Such a contingency plan as this could not have come from mindless and loveless evolution.

Prayer: I thank You, dear Father, for the ability to hear and read Your Word so that I can learn more about my Savior. Amen.

Ref: J.T. The Brain gets a (new) earful, Science News, November 14, 1999, v.154, p. 316

Barreleyes

Jeremiah 32:27

"Behold, I am the LORD, the God of all flesh: is there any thing too hard for me?"

Almost all sighted animals that aren't insects see with eyeballs. But that is not true of a fish named barreleyes, and that's for a good reason.

Barreleyes has that name because instead of eyeballs, the fish sees through tubes. The fish live a third of a mile below the surface, so studying them in detail was not possible until the last few decades. Barreleyes can move its eyetubes in different directions, depending on what it wants to look at. Even stranger, the eyetubes are *inside* the forehead and do not come into contact with the water at all. How can it see if its vision organs are inside its head? It has a transparent forehead filled with transparent liquid. What is the purpose of such a strange arrangement? Scientists believe that barreleyes eat siphonophores, which are jellyfish-like creatures that sting. The transparent forehead protects its eyes from getting stung.

Barreleyes' uniquely designed eyes are impossible to explain with gradual evolutionary modifications of regular fish eyes. Yet, they are well designed for barreleye's unusual way of making a living. As Scripture reminds us several times, nothing is too hard for God. As we read Scripture's record of what God has done in the past and what He has promised He still will do, especially for His people, this reminder is a comfort.

Prayer: Father, when I read of what You have promised me, remind me that nothing is too hard for You. Amen.

Ref: http://www.sciencenews.org/view/generic/id/41732, Susan Millius, "Barreleye peers at the world like a fighter pilot does through a windshield."

What Did History Do with the Dinosaurs?

Genesis 1:24

"And God said, Let the earth bring forth the living creature after his kind, cattle, and creeping thing, and beast of the earth after his kind: and it was so."

We are often asked why, if the Bible's account of creation is true, don't dinosaurs appear in any historical documentation. After all, according to the Bible, both the great land creatures and humans were created on day six of creation week.

The first thing to remember is that the term "dinosaur" is a modern term that has no historical usage. However, there are plenty of descriptions of dinosaur-like creatures throughout history. Virtually every culture has legends of dragons and other serpent-like creatures. The thunderbird of the America Indians sounds a lot like a flying reptile. This conclusion is supported by the fact that there are numerous rock carvings of what appears to be a flying reptile. Such carvings can be found in many places, including Arizona, Utah and Colorado.

Another rock carving in Utah resembles a long-necked dinosaur like an apatosaurus. It can be argued that Asia also had its share of dinosaurs. A carving found at an 800-year-old Cambodian monastery looks like a textbook depiction of a stegosaurus. But Central and South America seems to hold the record for dinosaur depictions. These include a man riding a dinosaur and a triceratops. Figurines have also been found in ancient graves that look like dinosaurs.

So history offers a good deal of witness to historical human contact with what we today call dinosaurs.

Prayer: Father, frustrate the efforts of those who would obscure and censor Your Holy Word and the history it presents. Amen.

Ref: *Acts & Facts*, 6/08, p. 13, John D. Morris, "The Dinosaur Next Door."

The Adder that Tells Time

Job 26:13

"By his spirit he hath garnished the heavens; his hand hath formed the crooked serpent."

Australia has many unique creatures that people find fascinating. One example is the floodplain death adder and its habit of eating dangerous frogs.

The marbled frog has a defense that could get the adder into trouble. It secretes an incredibly sticky mucus. If the adder gets some of this on himself, dirt, leaves and even sticks will begin to stick to him. When the adder strikes a marbled frog, he immediately drops the frog and waits. Studies show that two thirds of the stickiness of the mucus has degenerated by ten minutes after the frog dies. And that's how long the adder waits before he consumes the frog unharmed.

The Dahl's frog produces a powerful poison for its defense. The adder will quickly strike the frog and drop it so the adder's poison can kill it. Apparently, even this momentary contact is enough to deliver some poison to the adder. Scientists report that after such a strike the adder will writhe about. Eventually it recovers and continues to wait. After an average of 42 minutes, the adder eats the frog. Research shows that by this time the poison has degraded to nontoxic levels.

Researchers debate whether the adder's strategy of waiting different times for differing frog defenses is learned or inherited. We can be sure, however, that it was created.

Prayer: Father, I thank You for rescuing us from that old serpent, the devil, through Your Son, Jesus Christ. Amen.

Ref: *Science News*, 10/12/07, p. 227, S. Milius, "Eat a Killer."

Mystery Mountains Don't Have to Be a Mystery

Genesis 8:5

"And the waters decreased continually until the tenth month: in the tenth month, on the first day of the month, were the tops of the mountains seen."

There are three ways to make mountains. The movement of two crustal plates running into one another will push up mountains. Likewise, volcanic activity will produce mountains. Finally, massive erosion of soft strata from harder strata can also create mountains.

In the 1950s, Soviet researchers discovered a mountain range, named the Gamburtsev Mountains, in Antarctica. Since the mountain range lies under almost two-and-a-half miles of ice, they were discovered by seismic survey. There is one problem. There shouldn't be any mountains there, according to conventional science. That's because Antarctica is a single crustal plate colliding with nothing. Nor is there any evidence of volcanic activity there. As one scientist put it, finding these mountains is like opening an ancient pyramid and finding a living astronaut in it. However, there is another answer that uniformitarian geologists would never consider. We know that there was massive erosion as the flood waters drained from the earth, as evidenced by the Grand Canyon and the American Badlands. This would also seem to be the most likely explanation for the mystery mountains of Antarctica.

The Bible gives us the most accurate general history of the ancient Earth, actually filling in the gaps and contradictions that arise in modern long-age science approaches.

Prayer: Father, You judged the whole world in the flood. Remind my faith that You have judged me on the cross of Christ. Amen.

Ref: *Creation*, 3-5/09, p. 11, "Mountains that 'shouldn't be there.'"

Unknown Treasures Still Being Discovered

Proverbs 31:22

"She maketh herself coverings of tapestry; her clothing is silk and purple."

Many types of insects make silk. Among them, they make many types of silk. But many of the multitude of species of the caddisfly make a very unique silk even among silk-makers.

Many species of caddisfly larvae live underwater, which is where they spin their special silk. They spin silk to surround all but their head and four legs. Then they stick underwater debris like sand and bits of leaf to the silk. This helps camouflage them as they grow. It works so well that until recently scientists didn't realize that the caddisfly's protective cocoon was actually formed around silk. Perhaps you have already figured out what makes this silk unique. It is not only the only silk spun underwater, but it stays sticky despite the wet environment. Scientists are studying the chemistry of the silk to learn its secrets. What they learn could help them design a surgical tape for use in the body.

That we can learn so much from the creation bespeaks a Designer. If such designs were just the result of nature mindlessly stumbling upon these solutions, chances are that mankind would also have stumbled upon them by now, too. That we can learn such knowledge and apply it to problems we face is also among the treasures our Creator has placed in the creation for us.

Prayer: Father, I thank You that You have filled Your creation with so many treasures for us, including the treasure of knowledge. Amen.

Ref: http://www.laboratoryequipment.com/news-fly-glue-creates-bioadhesive-030110.aspx?xmlmenuid=5, 3/1/10 "Fly Glue Creates Bioadhesive."

Our Logic and God's Are Not the Same

Genesis 1:21a

"And God created great whales, and every living creature that moveth, which the waters brought forth abundantly..."

Ask any scientist and he'll tell you that blades designed to operate in fluids, like air or water, are best designed to have smooth edges. It only makes sense that a smooth leading edge is more efficient.

That's why, when a biologist noticed bumps on the front edge of a model of a humpback whale fin, he knew it had to be wrong. With some study, he discovered that the model was indeed accurate. The bumps are called tubercles. Testing has shown that the bumps result in an almost ten percent increase in the lift of a fin or blade. It decreases the drag of a blade or fin by one-third. In fact, one scientist concluded that the design is much better than "what [our] systems can accomplish." Inspired, scientists investigated whether similar tubercles could increase the efficiency of manmade blades such as those used on wind turbines. You may also find tubercles on helicopter blades and fan blades, as well.

While science can discover the excellency and superiority of God's design, it cannot learn of His spiritual wisdom by investigating the creation. That is revealed to us in Holy Scripture which tells us that He designed and created the whales as well as planning and carrying out His plan for our salvation through His Son, Jesus Christ.

Prayer: Father, I thank You for revealing the wisdom of Your salvation to me through Your Holy Word. Amen.

Ref: *Answers*, 4-6/09, p. 54, A. Peter Galling, "A Whale of a Design."

What the Cat Knew

Proverbs 16:23

"The heart of the wise teacheth his mouth, and addeth learning to his lips."

While modern computers can do increasingly amazing things, they would not compete well on even a simple task with an animal.

For example, you can teach a computer where the front door of your home is and where the furniture is in the living room. Give it wheels, park it at the front door and tell it to find the easy chair. No problem. Now move the furniture around and repeat the command to the computer. Now it is hopelessly lost. Move your furniture around, and the cat will still find your easy chair. Today's computers can do a few limited things that a cat's brain can do. But such a computer needs its own power supply and 140,000 central processing units. And even this arrangement is over 80 times slower than a cat's brain. In human and cat brains, memory and learning are possible because neurons are all connected to many other neurons. Thus, either a human or a cat can instantly recognize a familiar face. Engineers have invented a transistor replacement called a memristor which gives a computer the ability to learn and remember. Even using memristors, it would take a huge supercomputer with its own power supply much longer to recognize faces than we do.

Memory and the ability to learn is a gift of God, the source of all knowledge.

Prayer: Father, I thank You for giving me the ability to learn and then teaching me Your truth in Your Word. Amen.

Ref: http://www.ns.umich.edu/htdocs/releases/plainstory.php?id=763.3, University of Michigan News Service, 4/14/10, "Cat brain: A step toward the electronic equivalent."

Robot Without a Brain

Psalm 18:32

"It is God that girdeth me with strength, and maketh my way perfect."

A robot that can move about on its own must be programmed in great detail. Instructions must be given to each moving part. These instructions must also be able to direct the robot under all anticipated conditions. If there is any error in the instructions or an encounter with unexpected conditions, the robot will probably just freeze in place. Even slime mold can do better than this.

Even though slime mold cells are not connected to each other by nerves, when the cells join together, the resulting organism is able to move. It is able to deal with unexpected circumstances moving about by shifting liquid to change their collective bag-shaped body. Taking their cue from slime mold, a research group from Tohoku University in Japan has used the same principle to make a mobile robot. The robot is able to move across any flat surface by shifting liquid around, which changes pressure on different parts of the robot. It is made of 14 interconnected syringes, each with a motor to move the water. It moves around randomly until it is given a direction. Then the motors synchronize, and the robot begins to move in the commanded direction. This slime-mold type arrangement adjusts to changes in environment just like the real thing.

Leave it to God to accomplish a complicated task with a simple design.

Prayer: Father, move my heart to flee what will spiritually harm me and to seek that good You have to give me. Amen.

Ref: *Nikkei Weekly*, 9/13/10, p. 21. "Robot inspired by slime mold."

Beetle Produces Fungicide to Protect Young

Psalm 51:7

"Purge me with hyssop, and I shall be clean: wash me, and I shall be whiter than snow."

The southern pine beetle is a real problem in southeastern North America. They burrow into pine trees that could be harvested for lumber, often killing them. Those that aren't killed are left, stained an unattractive blue tint by a fungus they leave behind.

That fungus grows from spores carried in a special pouch under the beetles' neck. It will grow into a tiny garden that will feed the baby pine beetles when they hatch. However, several species of mite also infest the beetle. They have their own fungus that they use for food. That fungus will not sustain the baby beetles. Worse, the mite fungus is more robust than the beetle fungus and will crowd it out. However, the beetle also carries a special bacteria. The bacteria produces a very special fungicide. While it does not harm the beetle's fungus, it targets the mite's fungus, wiping it out. So, the baby southern pine beetle's little ones will have their fungus garden to feed them after all.

Natural fungicides and antibiotics surround us. The hyssop that God commanded His people to use in cleansing ceremonies is a natural antibiotic. While man has since learned to use many antibiotics, how did the beetle learn to use the right fungicide to protect its young? It should be clear that this relationship was arranged by our creating God.

Prayer: Father, I thank You that I have been cleansed from the filthiness of my sins through the blood of Jesus Christ. Amen.

Ref: http://www.sciencenews.org/view/generic/id/37160/title/beetles_grow_weed_killer, Susan Millius, "Beetles Grow Weed Killer."

See Who Is the Better Engineer?

Ecclesiastes 6:9
"Better is the sight of the eyes than the wandering of the desire: this is also vanity and vexation of spirit."

Scientists have always known that some brittlestars – relatives of the starfish – are sensitive to light. They can be observed avoiding predators and scampering into crevices for protection. However, it was not until recently that scientists discovered that brittlestars were actually able to see.

As scientists examined the brittlestars' transparent calcite skeletons, they found no obvious signs of eyes or other light-sensing structures. However, they did find what they called "an incredible array of spherical structures." Suspecting that these small structures might be lenses (since only brittlestars that respond to light have them), they investigated further. They were not prepared for what they found. They discovered that each of this multitude of spherical structures was a micro lens that focuses light to the tiny area of 3 micrometers across. That's about the size of the smallest particles of dust that you can see through a microscope! Because of the way in which calcite focuses light, each lens must be compound, actually being composed of two lenses. The resulting image is projected onto nerve fibers that feed into larger nerve bundles. Scientists noted that it is only recently that we have learned to make such micro lenses.

Such precision is no accident. But when men don't want to see God, they will see only the created – even when it comes to the origins of such precise, complex structures.

Prayer: Father, I rejoice at the wonders You have made. Help me never lose sight of them or salvation in Jesus Christ. Amen.

Ref: *Science News*, 8/25/01, p. 116, C. Schubert, "20/20 lenses coat body of sea creature."

Photosynthesis Without the Sun

Job 8:16

"He is green before the sun, and his branch shooteth forth in his garden."

We all learned about photosynthesis at school. For this particular chemical reaction to take place, you need the chemical chlorophyll, together with the essential ingredient – sunlight. For thousands of years, man has known that for green plants to prosper, they need the sunlight.

Now, a team of researchers from the University of British Columbia has discovered photosynthesis taking place nearly one-and-a-half miles below the surface of the sea. Of course, no sunlight penetrates to that depth, and that raises an interesting question. The creature performing this amazing task is a bacterium that has recently been discovered off the coast of Central America. So how can photosynthesis take place where there is no sunlight? These bacteria live around hydrothermal vents on the floor of the ocean. The vents spew out superheated water at about 570° Fahrenheit. As this water hits the cold ocean water, gas bubbles form and almost immediately collapse, producing a dim flash of light. Chemical reactions can also create a small amount of light, as does the formation of crystals under these conditions. Apparently, these bacteria are able to make enough energy to power their metabolism from these unlikely sources of light. However, it is difficult to imagine what possible evolutionary process could have given these bacteria that particular ability.

But God, knowing all things, can do the seemingly impossible just for His glory.

Prayer: Father, I rejoice and praise You, for all that You have made is fearfully and wonderfully made. Amen.

Ref: *Discover*, 1/06, p. 36, Anne Sasso, "Photosynthesizing Life-Form Exists Without Sunlight."

A Whale of a Song

Psalm 98:4

"Make a joyful noise unto the LORD, all the earth: make a loud noise, and rejoice, and sing praise."

Some have suggested a principle that there is a universal mathematics among living things. There appear to be some musical principles that illustrate this principle, called mathematical Platonism.

Humpback whales use rhythms in their songs that are like human music, even though they could use no rhythms at all. The phrasing in their songs lasts a few seconds, just as they do in human music, even though they could do much longer phrases. And like human music, the whales' songs repeat themes. The songs themselves typically run between the length of a human ballad and a symphony. They sing a theme, part of which they embellish, and then they go back to a modified version of the theme. While humpbacks are capable of singing over seven octaves, they actually sing notes that are similar in interval, or tone change, to human music. The whales are also capable of percussion in their songs, and they use it in about the same ratio as found in Western symphonies. Finally, like human music, the songs of humpbacks have repeating sections that create rhymes.

Whether these similarities may or may not be evidence of mathematical Platonism we don't know. But there is no question that the songs of whales glorify their and our Creator. May we praise our Lord for salvation, both here and in eternity.

Prayer: Lord, I praise you for the gift of music. Help me praise You for Your salvation, both here and in eternity. Amen.

Ref: *Science*, Vol. 291, 5/1/01, "The Music of Nature and the Nature of Music."

Stealthy Ants

James 5:20

"Let him know, that he which converteth the sinner from the error of his way shall save a soul from death, and shall hide a multitude of sins."

The Hirtella tree of French Guiana is very ant-friendly. A mature tree has hollow pouches at the base of their leaves that make comfortable ant apartments. In addition, it provides a sweet nectar for the ants.

Researchers studying the tree noticed that the tree typically had patches of gray mold growing on it. Looking a little closer, they discovered ants hiding in a leaf pouch underneath the mold. The ants had their mouths open and were looking out through holes in the mold. Scientists suspected that this was some sort of trap, so they placed various insects on the mold. Sure enough, the ants reached through the mold to hold and sting the insects. The ants' trick even worked with grasshoppers, which are much larger than the ants. Further research has shown that Hirtella trees without ants don't have the patches of mold. The ants find the mold, bring it to the trees and cultivate and trim it to make their traps.

The relationship between the Hirtella tree and the ants is amazing enough. However, the intelligence behind the ants' stealthy activity is even more amazing and could only come from an intelligent Creator. That Creator – Who taught the ants to do this – has sent His Son, Jesus Christ, so that our sins may be hidden from His sight and we could have forgiveness.

Prayer: Father, thank You for forgiving my sins through the saving work of Your Son and my Lord, Jesus Christ. Amen.

Ref: *Science News*, 4/23/05, p. 260, S. Milius, "Ambush Ants."

The Strangest Genetic Relationship

Daniel 4:3

"How great are his signs! and how mighty are his wonders! His kingdom is an everlasting kingdom, and his dominion is from generation to generation."

A very strange type of virus – that some scientists don't even think is a virus – depends on a parisitoid wasp for its existence. Without the wasp, it cannot even reproduce. Nor can the wasp reproduce without the virus.

The wasp is called a parisitoid wasp because it kills its host, whereas a true parasite does not kill its host. The drama begins almost unnoticed by a caterpillar as the small wasp stings it. Ten days later, the caterpillar stops moving but stays attached to whatever plant it's on. Then the eggs the wasp had injected with its sting begin to hatch, and the hatchlings begin eating their way out of the caterpillar. The question is, why didn't the caterpillar's immune system destroy the eggs? Because with the eggs, the wasp also injected the unusual virus that shut down the caterpillar's immune system. The only place the virus can reproduce is inside the wasp, where it does no harm. In fact, the relationship between the virus and the wasp is so close that its DNA has become part of the genetic structure of the wasp.

The relationship between the wasp and the virus is so close that it is obviously created. The evidence for this is especially clear since the virus is genetically dependent on the wasp.

Prayer: Lord, Your wonders are beyond counting, especially the wonder of Your plan of salvation through Your Son. Amen.

Ref: *Science News*, 2/26/05, pp. 136-137, David Shiga, "Poisonous Partnership."

Better Flower Power

1 John 1:8

"If we say that we have no sin, we deceive ourselves, and the truth is not in us."

On Creation Moments we have talked about a few orchids which fool bees and other pollinators so that they can reproduce. Actually, several hundred orchids have been discovered that fool pollinators with fake sexual signals. However, the champion deceiver has only recently been discovered, and it works its deception not only better, but differently than the others.

The species – known by its Latin name as O. speculum – looks something like the female of the wasp species that pollinates it. However, scent is its secret weapon. While most orchids that engage in such deception mix over a dozen chemicals to create the scent of the female of the species that pollinates it, this new orchid specializes. It creates only 10 chemicals, all of them rare, which the wasps respond to. One of these chemicals had only been seen before in honeybees. And while other orchids might attract only inexperienced pollinators, this new orchid will attract even experienced wasps. It does this by doing a better job of creating the wasp attractant than a female wasp can.

Obviously, orchids know nothing about chemistry and could not study the wasps before it needed a pollinator. This arrangement is clearly the work of a wise Creator, Who created both the wasps and the orchid.

Prayer: Father, help me not to be deceived by sin, but always place my trust in Jesus Christ for forgiveness. Amen.

Ref: *Science News*, 2/1/03, pp. 67-68, S. Milius, "Better Than Real."

The Jellyfish with 24 Eyes

Psalm 139:24

"Thine eyes did see my substance, yet being unperfect; and in thy book all my members were written, which in continuance were fashioned, when as yet there was none of them."

Many writers have pointed out that the claim that vision evolved gradually, over time, is difficult to believe. After all, there are many parts to the eye, there is the optic nerve, and there must be a portion of the brain that interprets what is seen. If any of these parts don't work, there is no vision, and no survival advantage.

However, evolutionists not only claim that vision evolved, but that it evolved several times. Because their vision systems are so different, evolutionists believe that vision evolved separately in cephalopods, vertebrates and the box jellyfish. Box jellyfish are better swimmers than most jellyfish, and some even have a courting ritual. A member of the family of box jellyfish has 24 eyes, six each on four different stalks. New research at Lund University in Sweden has shown that these eyes appear to be specialized. Eight of the eyes – two on each stalk – have lenses. Other eyes have irises that respond to light. Scientists believe that, despite all of these eyes, the box jellyfish sees only a blurry picture of its surroundings. However, it is able to see it in a wide-screen version.

Vision is a great blessing from God and a witness that all things are His handiwork. Some of His wonders have been formed so that we make no mistake about their origin.

Prayer: I thank You, Lord, that You have created such wonders. Help my life to glorify You, too. Amen.

Ref: *Science News*, 5/14/05, pp. 307-308, S. Milius, "Built for Blurs."

What Did They Really Look Like?

Proverbs 14:22

"Do they not err that devise evil? But mercy and truth shall be to them that devise good."

Drawings and models of extinct creatures, based upon fossil evidence, are usually referred to as reconstructions. Since no one has ever seen any of these creatures alive, just how accurate are the reconstructions of, say, the alleged ape-men now referred to by the politically correct as "pre-humans"?

A few years ago, *National Geographic* published the results of a study designed to answer this very question. Four different reconstruction artists were given casts of fossil bone pieces. The identical packages of fossil casts, they were told, were classified as Homo habilis. It was up to each artist to do his own research in reconstructing the original creature. Four different artists produced four very different reconstructions. Three of the reconstructions offered ground-living creatures, while one offered a tree dweller. Musculature differed among the reconstructions as did the amount of hair they had. Facial features spanned the range from very ape-like to almost human. What this experiment showed is that the reconstructions we see in magazines and museum displays that seem to support evolution are more art than science.

In a world filled with so much false perception and deception, we can be thankful for the Word of God, which is absolutely reliable as truth. Most importantly, it not merely shows us our sin, but reveals God's love for us in the forgiveness of sins in His Son, Jesus Christ.

Prayer: Father, I thank You for Your Word which is truth and which tells me of my Savior, Your Son, Jesus Christ. Amen.

Ref: *Creation*, 9-11/00, p. 6, "Artists' Impressions."

Ants' Play Red Light, Green Light

Psalm 119:105

"Thy word is a lamp unto my feet, and a light unto my path."

Scientists have long known that ants lay down scent trails, using pheromones, to mark the trail to goodies for their nest mates. While this is an efficient method for food gathering, it has recently been found that when a food source is exhausted, the ants leave a "Do not enter" sign that saves fellow ants wasting time on this trail.

While researchers were studying ant trails in the lab, they began to notice that some ants would make a U-turn about 15 ant-lengths before the fork in the trail that led to an exhausted food source. The researches believed that the ants can produce a repellant pheromone. So they set up a special test track that divided into two paths. Each ended at a feeder, but only one of the feeders had food. Each pathway had a removable paper cover. After the ants had used it for a while, establishing their trails, researchers moved the paper from the trail with no food to a new forked track. The trail that led to food received only a clean piece of paper. When the ants used the new experimental setup, 70 percent of them avoided the no-food trail.

Scientists had long rejected claims that ants foraged with this level of efficiency. However, why not admit that this efficiency, which had no reason to evolve, was intelligently created?

Prayer: Thank You, Lord, for Your Word that illuminates my life with Your love for me through my Lord, Jesus Christ. Amen.

Ref: *Science News*, 11/26/05, pp. 340-342, S. Milius, "Unway Sign."

This Song Defies Evolution

1 Chronicles 16:42

"And with them Heman and Jeduthun with trumpets and cymbals for those that should make a sound, and with musical instruments of God."

While many creatures create structured music – shall we say "songs"? – it was thought that only man makes use of objects in the environment to get specific tone qualities. In other words, it was thought that only man makes musical instruments. That claim has now been challenged by a frog!

Borneo's tree-hole frog is nowhere close to man on the evolutionary chart. Research shows that this frog searches out specific tree-holes filled with water. It is from such holes that the frog sits in the water and sings its song to attract females. Of course, these cavities – and the amount of water in them – vary from tree to tree, providing differing resonances from hole to hole. To deal with this, the frogs have been observed raising and lowering their pitch until they get a resonance. Once they find resonance, they begin singing in earnest. To test this, researchers placed a frog inside a pipe where they could change the water level, thus changing the resonance pitch. Every time they changed the water level, the frog would search for and find the new resonance pitch.

Evolutionary theory would never predict that a frog would learn how to use something in its environment as a musical instrument. However, the Bible says that music is a gift from our Creator Who can give it to any creature He wants.

Prayer: Thank You, Father, for the gift of music. Help me to use music to rejoice in Your salvation in Jesus Christ. Amen.

Ref: *Science News,* 12/7/02, p. 356, S. Milius, "Frogs Play Tree."

The Pre-Flood Atmosphere

Genesis 7:11b

"... the same day were all the fountains of the great deep broken up, and the windows of heaven were opened."

Listeners will know that fossil bones of some dinosaurs show that they were truly huge. In the same way, some of the flying reptiles – such as Pteranodon – were also truly huge, and this poses a problem. Bigger wings require bigger muscles, and eventually the creature is not going to get off the ground. Evolutionists agree that preservation of fossils means that they must have been rapidly buried, and Creation scientists point out that this could only have happened on a worldwide scale during the Genesis Flood. Creationists have theorized that before the Flood these very large flying creatures could have become airborne only if the air density was greater.

Evolutionists have often scoffed at such theorizing. However, after studies on rock oxidation, the chemistry of coal formation and other processes, the scoffing is now heard less often. Evolutionists agree that in the past – when millipedes were three-feet long and dragonflies were the size of hawks – there was more oxygen in the atmosphere. Their models show that this would indeed have resulted in increased air pressure, and they acknowledge that these conditions would have enabled larger creatures to survive.

The evolutionist begins with a theory, then applies well-founded scientific principles to explain the past. In contrast, Creation scientists begin with Scripture, then apply the same scientific principles to explain the past.

Prayer: I thank You, Father, that Your Word, which tells me of my Savior, is trustworthy in all things. Amen.

Ref: *Science News*, 12/7/05, pp. 395-396, Sid Perkins, "Changes In the Air."

Joseph's Amazing Coins

Genesis 41:40

"Thou shalt be over my house, and according unto thy word shall all my people be ruled: only in the throne will I be greater than thou."

Perplexed Pharaoh had dreamed of seven emaciated cows consuming seven well-fed cows by the Nile. Then he had the same dream involving ears of corn. None of Pharaoh's magicians could interpret his dreams. Then his cupbearer remembered Joseph, whom he had met in prison.

We all know how the story turned out. Joseph became second only to Pharaoh in ruling Egypt. The problem is, many scholars say that such stories, especially when they are from Genesis, are, at best, harmless folk tales. However, over years of excavations in Egypt, many small artifacts have been accumulated, documented, and then stored in the Cairo Museum of Egypt. Among those objects were round metal objects that many suggested were coins, though some scholars said these artifacts dated to a time before coinage was used for trade.

The objects have now been studied in detail. They are indeed ancient, dating to the time when Joseph was in Egypt as indicated by the minting date on them. They are clearly coins, bearing an inscription of their value. The coins even bear Joseph's name and an image which is probably his. One of the coins even bears the image of a cow, apparently commemorating Pharaoh's dream!

In Genesis, God gave us the first word on Joseph's story. Despite what some scholars say, God has had the last word in these artifacts.

Prayer: Father, I rejoice and thank You that Your Word, which tells me of my Savior and salvation, is trustworthy and true. Amen.

Ref: http://www.wnd.com/index.php?fa=page&pageId=111091, *World Net Daily*, 9/26/09, "Egyptian paper: Coins found bearing name of Joseph."

Hands Finger God as Creator

Acts 11:21

"And the hand of the Lord was with them: and a great number believed, and turned unto the Lord."

The human body is full of wonders. Many of these wonders are not understood by modern science. Some of these wonders, like your hands, are under our conscious control, and we can use them with precision; yet, science has difficulty fully explaining how they work.

Each of your hands has more than 30 muscles. From a mechanical standpoint, how your hand does what it does is difficult to explain. How your brain controls it with such precision is another mystery. In a study reported in *The Journal of Neuroscience,* researchers asked volunteers to tap and push their forefinger against a surface. As they did so, researchers measured the electrical activity in the hand. Bio-mechanically, this activity requires both force and push activities which are not mechanically compatible with each other. They concluded there must be some very specialized activity going on in the brain and nervous system just to tap your finger on a table and then push down. And the timing must be just right as your finger changes from move mode to push mode. This timing is very important. Without the proper timing from move to push you would not be able to pour or drink a glass of water.

Scripture often speaks of God's hand. Of course, being spirit He does not have physical hands except in the person of Jesus Christ.

Prayer: Thank You, dear Father, for all my gifts and abilities. Help me to use them to Your glory and the good of man. Amen.

Ref: *Creation*, March-May, 2009, p. 31, "Fingertip Control."

The Amazing Radio Ear

Joshua 3:9

"And Joshua said unto the children of Israel, Come hither, and hear the words of the LORD your God."

We all know there are AM radios as well as radios that can pick up both AM and FM. You may even have a shortwave radio, but each receiver must have a separate tuner for each set of frequencies. Cell phones, computer networks, television, the police and astronauts use a whole set of different frequencies. In fact, there are over a million frequencies, and for years no one ever hoped to have a single tuner that could receive them all.

Now that has all changed. MIT engineers with knowledge of both biology and radio were inspired by the design of the human ear as to how to build such an amazing tuner. The human ear has its own tuner that can receive frequencies between 100 hertz and 10,000 hertz. The ear's tuner is the cochlea, which has been described as a tuner that can receive 3,500 parallel channels at the same time. The engineers used the design of the cochlea to build a tuner that can receive and sort out more than a million frequencies at the same time. This tuner is on a computer chip that measures only 3 millimeters by one-and-a-half millimeters. This amazing receiver is called the radio frequency cochlea; it uses 100 times less energy than separate tuners over the same frequencies.

Again, modern engineers go to God's designs to improve our lives.

Prayer: Father, thank You for Your Word and its preaching. Prosper Your written and spoken Word in the hearts of all. Amen.

Ref: *TechTalk*, (MIT), 4/15/09, p. 4, Anne Trafton, "Drawing inspiration from nature to build a better radio."

Where Did Snake Venom Come From?

Genesis 3:18

"Thorns also and thistles shall it bring forth to thee; and thou shalt eat the herb of the field...."

God originally created the world without sin, and therefore without death. So how could poisonous snakes come into being, and how long did it take? Recent research into snake venoms offers some likely answers to these questions.

Snake venom is made primarily of proteins. The same family of proteins that make up snake venom is also common in chickens, mammals and humans. If you take a class of medications called A.C.E. inhibitors, you are actually putting proteins of this same venom family into your body. So why don't these kill us, when the bite of a pit viper which delivers the same class of proteins is fatal? The form of this family of proteins that make up venom is only slightly modified from the more common forms that we manufacture. However, those slight modifications make all the difference between a useful protein and venom. In one case it appears that a doubling of some genes that make a form of this protein caused the production of venom. How fast can such a common mutation happen? Apparently, rather quickly. Scientists have found that the same species of pit viper in Costa Rica have chemically different venom though only separated by a mountain range.

Scientifically we can say that it is likely that useful proteins were allowed to quickly mutate into venom after the fall into sin.

Prayer: Thank You, Father, for the remedy for sin in the innocent suffering and death of Your Son, Jesus Christ. Amen.

Ref: *Science News*, 8/15/09, pp. 16-20, Laura Sanders, "Venom Hunters."

The Most Unusual Winter Preparations in the World

Job 38:41

"Who provideth for the raven his food? when his young ones cry unto God, they wander for lack of meat."

Humans and animals that live in colder climates do different things to get ready for winter. One of the strangest preparations for cold weather is made by the Arctic Springtail.

Arctic Springtails are like centipedes but only a fraction of an inch long. When the Arctic temperatures are above freezing, Springtails live in mossy areas. That's where scientists collected them for study. They slowly chilled the Springtails to below freezing. This caused them to become darker in color, then shrivel up and finally go dormant. In fact, the Springtails looked so dried up that they appeared to be dead. This kind of preparation for the cold winter would kill most other creatures. However, the ability to completely dry out leaves no water in their body to form ice crystals that would then cause cell damage and kill the insect. When the Springtails were gradually warmed up, they rehydrated by absorbing water from melting ice and resumed activity. Scientists said that an understanding of what happens in the Springtails at freezing temperatures might help hospitals preserve transplant tissue.

Fossil forests show that the Arctic regions became cold very quickly so that this ability of the Springtail must have been built-in before the Arctic ice-age began. This little creature did not evolve by random processes. It was properly designed from the start by the Master Designer.

Prayer: Father, I thank You for the wondrous ways in which You provide for Your creatures. Amen.

Ref: *Science News*, 8/15/09, p. 9, Laura Sanders, "Springtail dries out for winter."

The Bird-Eating Spider

1 Samuel 17:4

"And there went out a champion out of the camp of the Philistines, named Goliath, of Gath, whose height was six cubits and a span."

Goliath, the giant whom David killed, was over nine feet tall. The Goliath tarantula spider also towers far above other species of tarantula.

Its full English name is the Goliath bird-eater, which might lead you to a question. The answer is, "Yes." While they have been seen eating earthworms and amphibians, one early specimen was observed eating a songbird. A native of French Guiana, the Goliath has a leg span of twelve inches and weighs in at a quarter of a pound. Its body is the size of a walnut, and its head is the size of a half dollar coin. Like other tarantulas, the Goliath's venom is not poisonous enough to kill a human.

It also has a second line of defense. It can kick microscopically barbed hairs from its abdomen that cause a burning irritation on bare skin. It also uses those hairs to make a hissing sound that can be heard ten feet away. Evolutionists had considered tarantulas insufficiently evolved to have any behaviors of interest. However, Goliath mothers have been seen allowing their children to eat freshly killed prey before they begin eating. Neither will they hurt another Goliath's youngsters, even if the are trying to get at their food.

The Goliath bird-eater's size glorifies God's creativity, while the behavioral characteristics He gave this creature contradict the expectations of evolution.

Prayer: Father, I marvel and praise You at the creativity and variety You have placed in the creation to Your Glory. Amen.

Ref: *Discover*, 2/04, pp. 62-67, Sy Montgomery, "Stalking Spiders."

The Beetle Born of Fire

Genesis 8:17b

"... and of every creeping thing that creepeth upon the earth; that they may breed abundantly in the earth, and be fruitful and multiply upon the earth."

Charles Darwin was an avid beetle collector, but the jewel beetle is one he never knew. First discovered in 1960, it has a very unusual lifestyle.

The female jewel beetle needs a good forest fire to reproduce. She will only lay her eggs on the bark of burned trees that may be still smoldering. There are a couple advantages to this need. First, after a forest fire, there are few, if any, predators around. Second, the burned tree cannot use its defenses against the infestation. But it would seem that there is one major obvious disadvantage to this manner of reproduction. Typically, a forest fire may not sweep through a given forest location within the lifetime of the beetle. Even though it can fly, it needs to find forest fire sites. So God has equipped the jewel beetle with infrared detection organs that can locate a forest fire up to 50 miles away. These tiny organs are found underneath the beetles' body. This ability to detect infrared radiation is so unusual that for decades scientists refused to believe that the beetle had this ability. After all, there is no evolutionary precedent for beetle infrared detection.

Of course, there doesn't need to be an evolutionary precedent since, as with all other creatures, it was designed for its lifestyle by an all-wise, all-powerful Creator.

Prayer: I rejoice, Father, in Your work of creation, and I praise You for the salvation You give me through Jesus Christ. Amen.

Ref: http://www.eurekalert.org/pub_releases/2004-07/uob-ffs072804.php

Eat Your Chocolate

Mark 7:15

"There is nothing from without a man, that entering into him can defile him: but the things which come out of him, those are they that defile the man."

A study by University Hospital in Cologne, Germany, just might bring both joy and improved health to some people. The study findings suggest that a small amount of chocolate can reduce blood pressure.

In the study, 44 Germans between the ages of 56 and 73 ate a small amount of dark chocolate every day for almost 5 months. The amount they ate was 6 grams – about the equivalent of one-and-a-half Hershey's kisses or 30 calories. Test subjects were instructed not to eat any other chocolate during the study. The result was that the participants' systolic blood pressure fell an average of three points while the diastolic blood pressure fell an average of two points. The 44 participants all had slightly elevated blood pressure. While the study is small, its results are similar to other studies of the effect of chocolate in the diet. The chocolate, it seems, relaxes blood vessels. Researchers warned that eating large amounts of chocolate and the resulting weight gain would counter any of the good effects a small amount of chocolate will have.

While modern science has a changing list of foods you should and should not eat, it is just beginning to get a more complete picture of nutrition. We can give God thanks that He has included tasty things that are good for us.

Prayer: Father, I thank You for all the good things You have given us, especially those that make our lives more enjoyable. Amen.

Ref: http://www.msnbc.msn.com/id/19587241/wid/11915773?GT1=10212

Learning from Fish

Luke 5:4

"Now when He had left speaking, He said unto Simon, 'Launch out into the deep, and let down your nets for a draught.'"

Many fish have a sensory organ called a lateral line. It runs along the length of a fish's body just under the skin. These organs are filled with sensitive hairs that sense the movement of water.

The organ gives a fish a better sense of speed and direction. It enables a school of fish to swim in synchronized fashion, allows it to locate and track prey and avoid predators and obstacles. Obviously, such a sensory system would be very useful for underwater robots and submarines. So researchers at the University of Illinois at Urbana-Champaign are trying to build an artificial lateral line. Their design is based on the structure of a fish's lateral line. It consists of micro-flow sensors arranged in a straight line. The artificial lateral line is able to detect some movement and vibration in water. Despite the best science and modern materials we have, the result so far is, the researchers admit, far inferior to that of the fish.

If our best minds using the range of modern materials available today cannot duplicate the precision of a fish's lateral line, it makes no sense to say that the fish's lateral line is the result of countless genetic accidents. The credit for the original design must go to the same God Who commanded the Galilean fish into the disciples' nets.

Prayer: Father, I thank You that Your handiwork is clear through the entire creation. Help me to bear witness of Your love. Amen.

Ref: http://www.news.uiuc.edu/news/07/0221fish.html

The Deceivers and the Deceived

1 Corinthians 3:18

"Let no man deceive himself. If any man among you seemeth to be wise in this world, let him become a fool, that he may be wise."

Blister beetle larvae have a unique way of getting themselves food, but they are also fussy about what they eat.

Blister beetle larvae prefer to eat pollen and wasp eggs. And they have a deceptively clever way to get to their lunch. They clump together on plants and emit a chemical that smells like a female wasp. This attracts a male wasp. When he gets close enough, they crawl on board the unsuspecting wasp. When he encounters a female wasp, the larvae transfer to her. They stay with her until she burrows up to six feet into sand. There she lays her single egg and leaves some pollen for her offspring to eat when it hatches. The egg and the pollen are enough to sustain the larvae until they emerge as fully grown beetles. It is difficult to argue that this clever deception is an accidental arrangement. Deception is not an unusual strategy among plants and animals. Previous Creation Moments have explored how some orchids emit female bee scents to attract male bees that will pollinate them. The female bolas spider emits scents that attract the male moths upon which it feeds.

Scripture warns us that those who think they are wise in the ways of the world have deceived themselves. Such worldly wisdom, such as belief in evolution, is said to be foolishness.

Prayer: Father, I ask Your protection from the deceptions of the evil one that I may always trust in Your mercy to me. Amen.

Ref: *Science News*, 9/16/06, pp. 181-182, S. Milius, "Sexually Deceptive Chemistry."

Can There Be Design Without a Designer?

Romans 1:20a

"For the invisible things of him from the creation of the world are clearly seen, being understood by the things that are made, even his eternal power and Godhead..."

A new science called biomimetics is making news. In the past we have talked about how some of man's designs are often similar to God's which do the same job. However, in biomimetics, researchers actively seek to study the creation to learn of designs that will solve engineering problems.

We are all familiar with the story of how thistle seeds inspired Velcro. Engineers have used the design of the owl's wing to make the structures that carry electrical current to trains. The result is a much quieter ride. The moth's eyes' ability not to reflect light helps make it harder to be spotted by birds. The same design has now been used to make a nonreflective film. The result is a film that can be used to help prevent windows from reflecting light. This film will soon be available commercially. Many dyes are toxic, yet many creatures manage to show off bright colors without using toxic substances. Materials engineers studied how the jewel beetle produces its color. The result is a film that seems to change color depending on the angle from which you view it.

No scientist can offer a rational explanation for how so many thoughtful and efficient designs could be generated in a mindless universe. These designs are fingerprints God left all over the creation so that man might seek Him out.

Prayer: I thank and praise You, dear Father, for the excellence and wonder You have left as fingerprints in the creation. Amen.

Ref: *Nikkei Weekly*, 2/22/10, p. 17, "Biomimetics yields life-inspired products."

The Fastest Jaws in the World

Psalm 46:7

"The LORD of hosts is with us; the God of Jacob is our refuge."

If an octopus thinks you have found him in his lair, he will squirt ink in your face and hope, in your surprise, you don't see him fleeing. On the other hand, challenge a bull, and you will have more fight on your hands than you want. Other creatures will evaluate the situation to determine whether fight or flight is the best response.

The trap-jaw ant has a unique approach to this problem of fight or flight. He can fight, flee or do both at the same time with the same movement. The ant has a unique mandible. It is this jaw that is the secret of the ant's response to a challenge. If the ant faces a threat and decides to attack, it will strike at the threat with its mandibles and in the movement propel itself up to nine inches from the threat almost simultaneously. If the ant decides to flee, it simply does so by snapping its jaws shut against the ground on which it stands. Its jaw snaps closed at the speed of over 136 miles per hour.

While it is sometimes necessary to protect ourselves from earthly dangers through fight or flight, neither of these will work for the spiritual dangers we face. For those we must trust the strong arm of our risen Savior.

Prayer: Lord, You are our protecting fortress when danger threatens. Help us to trust You in every situation. Amen.

Ref: *Photonics Spectra*, 12/06, p.154, Lauren I. Rugani, "Self-Propelling Picnic Pests."

The Real King Solomon's Mines

2 Samuel 8:14a

"And he put garrisons in Edom; throughout all Edom put he garrisons, and all they of Edom became David's servants."

There is a school of biblical interpretation that does not consider the Bible divinely inspired. For example, they say that the Bible's description of David's conquests and Solomon's wealth and greatness were written down many centuries after they lived. The stories had been verbally passed down, getting wildly exaggerated through the years. When they lived, Israel and Edom were little more than a few small, insignificant tribal villages.

Over the years, various archaeological finds have challenged this view in support of the biblical account. New findings have again supported the biblical history. Scripture describes David's conquests as having included Edom, which became a servant state to him. In the 1930s, the famous pioneer Holy Land archaeologist Nelson Glueck claimed to have discovered King Solomon's mines in what was the northern part of Edom. Now more complete excavations have been done in the northern part of Edom near the claimed mines and have revealed that there was extensive copper production taking place in the area. What's more, artifacts and several dating methods have left no doubt that copper production was taking place at the site during David's and Solomon's time.

As we've often said, we don't believe the Bible because of scientific proof of its truth, but we do expect it to be accurate.

Prayer: Father, do not allow those who doubt Your Word to fool Your people. Convince them of the truth of Your Word. Amen.

Ref: *Science News*, 11/22/08, p. 10, Bruce Bower, "David, Solomon may have been kings of copper."

Self-Cleaning Feet

Psalm 148:7, 10

"Praise the LORD from the earth, ye dragons, and all deeps ... Beasts, and all cattle; creeping things, and flying fowl...."

Here on ***Creation Moments*** we have often mentioned the gecko's amazing ability to walk up, or even upside down, on surfaces as smooth as glass. We have pointed out that the gecko can grip even a glass surface as it walks with microscopic hairs on its feet. These minute hairs actually grip the surface at the molecular level.

Noting that geckos never seem to clean their feet, scientists wondered what would happen if the microscopic hairs became fouled with microscopic dust particles. They computed that particles would have to foul between 26 and 59 hairs on each foot to be effective. They then fouled geckos' feet with micro-spheres and observed them as they walked on a glass surface. To their surprise, with each step the geckos' grip on the glass surface became stronger. This result suggested that with each step, the geckos' feet were shedding some of the micro-spheres. To determine if this was what was happening, scientists removed some of the fibers from gecko feet and studied their interaction with the micro-spheres. Their conclusion was that gecko feet are indeed self-cleaning.

Not only is the design of the gecko's feet amazing, but God evidently realized that His design would not work unless it was self-cleaning and able to shed dust. This design certainly cannot be attributed to a hit or miss process like evolution.

Prayer: Father, with all You have made, I praise You, not only for my being, but also for my redemption in Christ. Amen.

Ref: *Science News*, 1/8/05, pp. 21-22, P. Weiss, "Twinkle Toes."

Some Dinosaurs Ate Grass!

Job 40:15

"Behold now behemoth, which I made with thee; he eateth grass as an ox."

The Genesis creation account tells us that in the perfect world that God created there was no death. This means that there were no predators. In fact, Genesis 1:30 specifically states that God gave all the beasts and birds every green herb for food. And, yes, this would include all the dinosaurs. Some discoveries made in 2005 now add strong scientific evidence to support the Genesis account that in the beginning all the beasts ate the green herbs for food.

Of course, evolutionists found great amusement in these Bible claims since even plant-eating dinosaurs didn't have the right kind of teeth to eat, say, grass. And besides, they said, grass did not evolve until long after the dinosaurs were extinct. Scientists from India's Birbal Sahni Institute of Palaeobotony examined fossilized sauropod droppings to see what they were eating. Common in such droppings are bits of silica called phytoliths. These bits of silica were the remains of the plants eaten by those dinosaurs, and are unique to each species of plant. To the surprise of the entire scientific community, the phytoliths were made by grasses, including relatives of rice, bamboo and forage grasses.

It is now unquestionably clear that grasses did exist when the dinosaurs lived, and that the sauropods ate grass. On this fact the Bible was right all along, and evolutionary science was wrong.

Prayer: Father, I thank You that Your Word is true in all that it teaches, including my salvation is Jesus Christ.

Ref: *Minneapolis Star Tribune*, 11/18/05, p. A4, Lauren Neergaard, "Rewriting prehistory: Dinosaurs had their grass and ate it, too."

Ants Go Homeless for Cheating

2 Corinthians 8:21

"Providing for honest things, not only in the sight of the Lord, but also in the sight of men."

Many plants give ants special protection and in return, the ants protect these plants from other insects. In itself, this widespread arrangement offers evidence of design. However, sometimes these arrangements are even more complex than they at first appear.

A small tree that grows in the central Amazon of Brazil, called the *Hirtella,* offers small ants shelter in tiny pouches that form in pairs at the base of young leaves. Scientists prevented the ants from reaching some of the branches of a tree and noted that those branches lost about half of their new foliage to other insects. It appeared that the ants were keeping other pests off the new growth in return for shelter. However, scientists also found that the branches that had no ants also had eight times as many flowers as those branches the ants could reach. Apparently, the ants do a good job at protecting new growth, but once flowers begin to form the ants become the pests. The *Hirtella* doesn't ignore this. Once the new foliage is established and it is time to flower, the leaves drop the ant shelters so that the ants have to find somewhere else to call home.

This elegant defense arrangement is clear testimony not only to God's design, but also His provision for a complex creation with a vast array of creatures.

Prayer: Father, surround me with honest people, and help me to be honest so that my life reflects what I have in Christ. Amen.

Ref: *Science News*, 11/2/02, p. 285, "Ant cheats plant; plant cheats back."

"The Most Perfect Design I've Ever Seen"

Psalm 107:24

"These see the works of the LORD, and his wonders in the deep."

"The most perfect design I've ever seen." Those words were uttered by a materials engineer after studying a deep sea sponge from the Pacific Ocean. And, indeed, the *Euplectella aspergillun*, claimed to be an early and primitive sponge, can teach modern materials engineers a number of useful things.

The sponge's body is made up of a thin layer of cells over an intricate glass skeleton. The sponge grows into a cylindrical shape about 8 inches long and about an inch across. The wonder lies in the glass skeleton that is made up of vertical and horizontal beams of glass. Diagonal beams strengthen this grid. One-third of these beams are thicker than the others, adding the extra strength of ridges to the cylinder. What's more, each of these glass beams is made up of small cylinders of glass glued together with more glass-like tree rings. The result is a structure that spreads the pressures that might crush an ordinary glass structure this size. It is a delicate looking, but nearly unbreakable, glass structure. In a less than scientific test, one researcher noted that one has to jump full weight on one of these cylinders to even produce any cracking, and such jumping will still not break it.

"The most perfect design I've ever seen." There's little we at ***Creation Moments*** can add to that.

Prayer: Father, I thank You for all Your wonders, the greatest of which is Your love in forgiving me for Jesus' sake. Amen.

Ref: *Science News*, 3/25/06, pp. 184-185, Aimee Cunningham, "Making the Most of It."

The Worm Turns on Plants

Psalm 59:17

"Unto thee, O my strength, will I sing: for God is my defense, and the God of my mercy."

Regular listeners to ***Creation Moments*** are familiar with the many examples we have described of plants protecting themselves from insects.

A wide variety of plants make self-defense insect poisons by first producing the chemical jasmonate. Consideration was being given by the insecticide industry to stimulate plant defenses by spraying crops with this naturally occurring chemical. However, research now shows that this might not be a good idea. A worm, known variously as the corn earworm, the cotton bollworm or the tomato fruit worm, infests more than 100 plant species. This worm has two amazing abilities that probably explain why it's such a pest. First, it can sense when a plant begins to produce jasmonate, the first step in production of its self-defense poisons. When the worm senses jasmonate, it produces enzymes that will detoxify those plant's poisons. Studies have shown that spraying crops with jasmonate will only tip off the worm's detoxification abilities, and make it more resistant to the plant's self-defense poisons. It appears that the plants rely on surprise to discourage the worms.

Of course, neither the plants nor the worms know anything about chemistry. It is the Creator of heaven and earth, Who has given both the worm and the plants their defense mechanisms and, through His Son, Jesus Christ, has offered mankind protection from sin, death and the devil.

Prayer: Father, I thank You for the protection from sin, death and the devil that I have in Your Son, Jesus Christ. Amen.

Ref: *Science News*, 10/19/02, p. 246, S. Milius, "Spying on Plant Defenses."

Life from Blood

Genesis 9:4

"But flesh with the life thereof, which is the blood thereof, shall ye not eat."

The Bible teaches us that our physical life is in our blood. It also teaches us that our spiritual and eternal life is dependent upon the blood of Jesus Christ.

Your heart pumps blood at a speed of more than three feet per second. This means that any given red blood cell will make a full circulatory trip from your lungs and back in only about a minute. But your heart is not the only hard working part of your circulatory system. Your red blood cells live only about 4 months. In that time, a red blood cell has made over 170,000 trips from your lungs to bring oxygen to every part of your body. That means your body must constantly replace red blood cells. So your body produces about 2 million new red blood cells every second. Your body does this most efficiently by recycling the iron from dead red blood cells into the new red blood cells. Iron, of course, gives the hemoglobin in red blood cells the ability to carry oxygen.

As we learn more about our circulatory systems, we see that physical life is a daily gift from God. Yet, it was the life-blood of our Savior, Jesus Christ, shed on the cross for us in His holy, innocent suffering and death that makes eternal life possible for us.

Prayer: Lord Jesus Christ, thank You for shedding Your life-blood on the cross so that I am forgiven and accepted by God. Amen.

Ref: *Science News*, 6/3/06, pp. 346-348, Ben Harder, "Blood, Iron, and Gray Hair."

Another Evolution Claim Goes Extinct

1 Corinthians 2:13a

"Which things also we speak, not in the words which man's wisdom teacheth, but which the Holy Ghost teacheth...."

Evolutionists regularly announce that they have scientifically proven that this creature evolved from that creature. Or they say that science proves that this creature or that one has been extinct for millions of years. Further, such claims are not to be questioned because they have been proven by science.

It's been well over a century since Darwin laid the foundation for these claims. Since that time, whole books have been written about how the alleged claims of scientific proof have, themselves, been proven wrong. Today, we add one more discovery to the list of unproven claims. Evolution claims that the Diatomydae, commonly known as the rat-squirrel, has been extinct for eleven million years. That is, until freshly caught rat-squirrels were found for sale at a meat market in Laos. The creatures have a rat-like face with a squirrel-like body and a not-very-bushy tail. They are smaller than the common squirrel. A careful analysis of the fossils and the skeletons of the modern specimens have convinced scientists that they are indeed the same creature. The rat-squirrels live deep in the forests of Laos seldom visited by Westerners.

Man's wisdom has given birth to the theory of evolution. God's wisdom, the heart of which is the Gospel of salvation in Jesus Christ, naturally contradicts man's wisdom where man is wrong. You can count on it.

Prayer: Father, I thank You for Your wisdom in Your Word. Help Your wisdom to dispel man's wisdom in my life. Amen.

Ref: *USA Today*, 3/9/06, Mark A. Klinger, "Rat-squirrel not extinct after all."

Hummingbird Wristwatches

Psalm 25:6

"Remember, O LORD, thy tender mercies and thy lovingkindnesses; for they have been ever of old."

When you remember something that happened, and where and when it happened you are using what scientists call episodic memory. Scientists have traditionally thought that such memory was unique to man.

Other scientists suspected that possibly some creatures may have episodic memory. For example, take the hummingbird with its fast metabolism. They need to eat often and remember where reliable sources of nutrition are to be found. At the same time, different flowers regenerate nectar at different rates. Researchers went to the natural habitat of the rufous hummingbird, equipped with some fake flowers and sugar water. The manmade flowers were constructed with reservoirs that could hold the sugar water. Half the flowers were refilled ten minutes after a bird would feed from it, while the other half were refilled twenty minutes after a feeding. Researchers found that the birds quickly learned which flowers were filled at which intervals. They soon returned to the flowers that were filled every ten minutes at ten-minute intervals while they waited twenty minutes in between visits to the other flowers. They noted that the birds did a good job of this even though they were keeping track of eight flowers.

It makes more sense to believe that episodic memory is a sophisticated ability that is the gift from a caring God to those creatures whom He knew would need it.

Prayer: Father, never let me forget Your love to me through Jesus Christ, Your Son. Amen.

Ref: *Science News*, 4/15/06, p. 237, "Hummingbirds can clock flower refills."

Doctor Lobster?

Leviticus 13:8

"And if the priest see that, behold, the scab spreadeth in the skin, then the priest shall pronounce him unclean: it is a leprosy."

The spiny lobster is a social creature. Lobsters like to congregate in groups in crevices and cooperate in defending their home against danger. When they migrate, they walk head to tail in single file groups.

However, researchers have noted that certain lobster lairs contained only one lobster. They also noted that some of these loners did not appear healthy. Upon further study, they found that the lobsters that looked unwell were infected with a virus they named PaV1. That virus, they learned, is commonly spread by physical contact, although young lobsters can be infected through water contaminated with the virus. Further, underwater surveys revealed that even when the disease is not apparent, healthy lobsters avoid those infected with the virus. While 56 percent of the healthy lobsters were found sharing a lair, only 7 percent of the infected lobsters shared living space. In lab tests, 60 percent of the healthy lobsters avoided a hiding place it if had an infected lobster in it. Scientists don't know how the healthy lobsters can sense the virus, but it is obvious that they do and they avoid their sick comrades.

Before the advent of modern medicine, people knew to avoid others with obvious diseases like leprosy. It appears that God also gave the same ability to sense disease and avoid contact with it to the lowly lobster.

Prayer: Father, I thank You for the blessings of modern medicine. But I thank You more for the healing I have in Christ. Amen.

Ref: *Science News*, 5/27/06, pp. 325-326, S. Milius, "Lobster Hygiene."

Trying to Spin an Evolutionary History Out of Spider Silk

Job 8:13-14

"So are the paths of all that forget God; and the hypocrite's hope shall perish: Whose hope shall be cut off, and whose trust shall be a spider's web."

Scientists recently examined a well-preserved spider web encased in amber. It is the oldest example of a spider web in existence and was declared to be one-hundred and ten million years old.

The researchers were eager to find out what the specimen might teach them about spider evolution. The web consisted of 26 strands of silk preserved in the amber while the pattern of the web appeared to be just like that of the modern orb-weaving spider. Three insects that were held by the web when it was encased in amber were also preserved. Interestingly, these three insects: a wasp, a fly and a mite, are the same three insects that are most often caught by modern orb spiders. Today's orb spiders place drops of glue along their web to capture their insects. The composition of the ancient glue and the modern glue were the same, however, it turned out that the ancient spider had applied the glue in a slightly different way from its modern cousin. From this small detail the researchers tried to spin an evolutionary tale about this spider. Mankind the world over uses different techniques to achieve the same purpose.

The fact remains that the ancient spider's web design and way of making a living was identical to that of modern spiders. There was certainly no evidence of evolution here.

Prayer: Lord, help me to more clearly see Your hand in Your creation and remember Your mercies to me every day. Amen.

Ref: *Science News*, 6/24/06, p. 390, S. Perkins, "Sticky Subjects."

Electric Singing and Arguing

Genesis 1:20a

"And God said, Let the waters bring forth abundantly the moving creature that hath life ...."

The brown ghost knifefish, popular in many aquariums, generates a weak electric signal that it uses for navigation and communication. The electric field they generate is too weak to stun prey. However, the electric organs that run along the sides of their bodies can pick up any changes in the field when the field encounters something with a conductivity that is different than water.

The communication aspects of the field are even more amazing. Male knifefish have been recorded singing to females by modulating their electric field. Researchers report that the males will sing like this for hours at night. However, when two knifefish who are hostile to one another encounter each other, they will raise the frequency of their electric field to jam their rival's signal. Researchers confirmed their conclusion that the knifefish were attempting to jam an enemy's signal by using a dummy knife fish. They rigged the dummy to generate signals that mimicked a knifefish. Then they placed two male knifefish in the tank with it. The two males were rivals to the dummy and both male knifefish quickly raised their frequencies to jam the rival's signal.

Some people believe that mindless evolution gave the knifefish the ability to generate and control electric fields for communication, as well as the ability to receive those signals. That credit clearly belongs to God!

Prayer: Father, I thank You that You have communicated Your love for me through the Gospel of Jesus Christ. Amen.

Ref: *Science News*, 11/19/05, pp. 324-325, S. Milius, "Tszzzzzt!"

You Can't Hear This Surprise

Psalm 5:3

"My voice shalt thou hear in the morning, O LORD; in the morning will I direct my prayer unto thee, and will look up."

The concave-eared torrent frog of China sings like a bird with a wide assortment of whistles and chirps. They live where streams and rivers splash down rocky mountainsides.

Researchers got a surprise when they were studying sonograms of the frog's singing that they had recorded on equipment used to study bats. The sonograms revealed strong signals above 20 kilohertz, and way above human hearing range. So scientists wondered, can the frogs hear such ultrasonic signals? To find out, they went to the frogs' habitat with equipment designed to record and play the full range of their songs. They then played the ultrasonic songs they had recorded. One of the native male frogs quickly responded. To verify that the frogs could actually hear the ultrasonic calls, researchers then placed electrodes into the portion of the frog's brain that processes hearing. Sure enough, the frog was hearing the ultrasonic calls. Further testing showed that the frogs can hear sounds as high-pitched as 34 kilohertz. They then realized that this makes perfect sense. The water splashing over the rocks in their habitat creates a lot of white noise, so the frogs need to communicate in sound frequencies well above that of the surrounding white noise.

This unique design reminds us that God cares for all of His creatures and has fully prepared each kind for survival.

Prayer: Thank You, Father, that You have promised to always hear the prayers of Your children in Christ. Amen.

Ref: *Science News*, 3/18/06, pp. 165-166, S. Milius, "Can You Hear Me Now?"

A Real Crime-Fighting Bat

Mark 4:22

"For there is nothing hid, which shall not be manifested; neither is any thing kept secret, but that it should come abroad."

Airport security is a major concern these days. There are many ways for those who don't have good intentions to hide things beneath their clothes. Now, thanks to a design they borrowed from our Creator God, scientists have come up with a way to make that virtually impossible,

The new security device, is called Tadar, and uses harmless high frequency waves to create images on a screen. The high frequency waves have a wavelength of only 3 millimeters. These waves reflect from anything that is blocking a person's natural radiation. This means that anything hidden under someone's clothing will be seen on the Tadar's screen. The screen itself provides ten 3-dimensional images per second. Tadar can see anything from a metal gun to plastic explosives, since any object will obstruct some of the body's natural radiation. Tadar is also not invasive and can pick up objects hidden behind clothing up to 160 feet away. Tadar is named after the Brazilian bat, *Tadarida brasiliensis*, which uses the same high frequency pulses to find its prey.

The more sophisticated our technology becomes, the more obvious it becomes that the living things around us are not the product of chance. But while science can show us the hand of the Creator, only Scripture tells us of His love for us by sending His Son to save us.

Prayer: Father, I thank You that Your love for me is not hidden. It is shown to me in the death and Resurrection of Jesus. Amen.

Ref: *Photonics Spectra*, 12/05, p. 172, "Bat Patrol."

Cooked Wasps

Psalm 82:3

"Defend the poor and fatherless: do justice to the afflicted and needy."

Domesticated honeybees in China are preyed upon by a native wasp. A single wasp can wipe out a nest of 6,000 bees before carrying off the larvae to feed its own young. The wasp does this by stationing itself at the entrance to the nest and killing the guards one by one as they come out to defend the hive.

However, the Chinese honeybees are not defenseless. If enough of them can get to a wasp they will literally coat the wasp. Research shows that they are doing something even more effective than stinging it. They are cooking the wasp to death. Bees generate heat by shivering their flight muscles. Both European and Chinese honeybees use this strategy to heat their nest when it gets cold. Researchers found that a wasp, fully encased in honeybees, will be heated to 113 degrees (F), in five minutes, enough to kill the wasp. European and Asian honeybees can stand temperatures over 120 degrees. However, the Asian bees must muster half again as many bees to cook the wasp.

In God's foreknowledge, He knew that man's eventual sin would affect the entire creation. So He gave the creatures of His creation the ability to defend themselves. Likewise, He protects us from sin, death and the devil through the forgiveness of sins that is ours through Jesus Christ.

Prayer: Father, I thank You for Your protection from sin in Jesus Christ. Help me to protect the weak. Amen.

Ref: *Science News*, 9/24/05, p. 197, S. Milius, "Balls of Fire."

Photosynthesis in the Dark

Psalm 136:4

"To him who alone doeth great wonders: for his mercy endureth for ever."

A new bacterium that grows at depths of over 8,000 feet below the ocean's surface has been discovered. This discovery wouldn't normally be very noteworthy except for the fact that none of the sun's light reaches that depth, yet the bacterium makes its living through photosynthesis.

The emerald green organism was discovered off the Mexican coast in the Pacific Ocean. Named GSB1, the bacterium is what is classified as a green sulfur bacterium. These organisms thrive in a low oxygen, high sulfur environment. Those are the conditions found in deep-sea hydrothermal vents known as black smokers. These vents spew sulfur-rich, low oxygen hot water as hot as 750 degrees (F). Just as a hot stove burner emits a small amount of light, water this hot also emits a small amount of visible light. Most of the light is infrared, which cannot be used for photosynthesis. The visible portion of the light is so dim that it cannot be seen except through night goggles. Yet the bacterium manages to perform photosynthesis in this very dim glow. This is the only known organism that performs photosynthesis without sunlight.

We are still learning about the wonders of God's unlimited creativity. However, His greatest wonder is His love, which led Him to send His only Son, Jesus Christ, to redeem us from sin, death and the devil.

Prayer: Father, I praise you for all Your wonders, especially the wonder of Your love and salvation. Amen.

Ref: *Science News*, 6/25/05, pp. 405-406, N. Moreira, "Grow in the Dark."

Plant Sniffs Out Prey

Psalm 104:14

"He causeth the grass to grow for the cattle, and herb for the service of man: that he may bring forth food out of the earth...."

The dodder is a very unusual plant and is known as one of the ten worst weeds found in the United States. A newly sprouted dodder seed does not bother to grow roots. Rather, it sprouts a tendril that grows out, looking for other plants. It has, at most, a week to find a plant from which to steal water and nutrients.

The dodder is a parasite and while it does not kill its victims, it will take enough water and nutrition to stunt their growth. The dodder actually costs California tomato growers $4 million dollars a year in losses. Researchers found that the species of dodder that causes most trouble to tomato plants actually "sniffs out" its victims. Scientists knew that plants emit pheromones or scents unique to each species. The researchers gave a sprouting dodder seed a choice of targets to grow toward, including a tomato plant. When the dodder seed sprouted it immediately sent a tendril out to the tomato. In a more rigorous test, researchers connected possible targets in separate enclosures to the sprouting dodder with curved tubes. The dodder still found the tomato plant.

The dodder has no nervous system and scientist's marvel at what it can do. Rather, they should be marveling at what our Creator can do in providing for the needs of all living things.

Prayer: Father, I thank You for supplying our daily bread as well as our eternal salvation. In Jesus' Name. Amen.

Ref: *Science News*, 9/30/06, p. 214, S. Milius, "Scent Stalking."

Smart Mollusks

Job 21:22

"Shall any teach God knowledge? seeing he judgeth those that are high."

According to modern thinking, intelligence is a product of several factors. Of course, the most important requirement is that the creature must be high on the evolutionary tree. Intelligence is also related to life span, the longer the better, and the fact that they are social creatures.

However, don't tell this to a group of creatures who are considered very low on the evolutionary tree, for they have very short life spans and are usually solitary. Various studies are showing that octopuses, cousin to the lowly clam, are among the most intelligent creatures on earth. Researchers have found that octopuses not only learn how to solve problems like mazes, but remember what they learn. They report that at one marine lab, some octopuses would sneak out of their tanks at night to eat fish in other tanks. But more indicative of intelligence is the fact that octopuses show personality. Different individuals may, for example, react to an unfamiliar item with curiosity, fear, or even by attacking it. Another indication of intelligence is play. Octopuses will play with floating objects in their tanks in much the same way as a child will play with floating toys in the tub.

None of the traditional evolutionary explanations for intelligence apply to the octopus. Actually, none of those explanations apply to any creature, since all received their intelligence from our Creator.

Prayer: Father, I thank You for intelligence, help me to use it wisely to number my days on earth. Amen.

Ref: *Discover*, 10/03, pp. 46-51, Eric Scigliano, "Through the Eye of an Octopus."

You Need a Healthy Laugh

Proverbs 17:22

"A merry heart doeth good like a medicine: but a broken spirit drieth the bones."

Laughing is good for you even if it does begin with the release of adrenaline and other stress hormones.

Whether you are tickled or reacting to a good joke, at least seven different centers in the brain react in various ways. Your response begins with the release of stress hormones. Your normal breathing rhythm gets interrupted and various neurotransmitters, including dopamine are released. And, yes, your brain also interprets the tickle so that you cannot tickle yourself since your brain knows when your own fingers are involved. Scientists also believe that as you begin laughing, your saliva glands begin to secrete extra immune compounds. Antibodies and virus killing T-cells are also released in larger doses. Your heart beats also increase and your blood pressure goes up to support the muscle spasms that result from your laugh. Those muscle spasms are actually a good aerobic exercise. In fact, one minute of a good laugh is said to be as good as ten minutes of exercise on a rowing machine!

Besides promoting social bonds, laughing is indeed good for you in many ways. Tickling is common way that parents bond with their young children. And wholesome humor can cheer the heart and raise the spirits. Moreover, while laughing appears to have no evolutionary advantage, it is easily explained as a gift of God to raise our spirits.

Prayer: Father, I thank You for the gift of laughter. Help me to use humor and laughing in a wholesome way. Amen.

Ref: *Discover*, 4/03, pp. 62-69, Steve Johnson "Laughter."

What We Don't Know

Job 38:2-3

"Who is this that darkeneth counsel by words without knowledge? Gird up now thy loins like a man; for I will demand of thee, and answer thou me."

When we read biology textbooks or watch television programs about science and discovery we are led to believe that evolution is not a theory but a scientifically established fact. We are told with great confidence how life first arose on the ancient earth, or when each species first evolved and the precise evolutionary relationships between different creatures. And, of course, the impression is given that all of this is established beyond question.

But is that what scientists themselves are telling each other behind the closed walls of academia? In 2005, the scientific journal, ***Science,*** celebrated its 125th anniversary. As part of their celebration, they listed 125 questions that science has not answered. One of the questions was, "How and where did life on earth arise?" Apparently scientists have not established the origin of life as a fact. Another question they said that science has not answered was, "What determines species diversity?" If this question has not been answered by science, how can science describe the history of the various species and their evolutionary relationships?

It would seem that the origin and evolution of life are not scientifically established facts, despite how these are portrayed in textbooks and on television. These Godless and fraudulent claims made for what is still the theory of evolution should not be allowed to deceive us and our children.

Prayer: Father, I thank You for Your revealed truth in Holy Scripture. Guide us so that none are misled by the world. Amen.

Ref: *World*, 7/23/05, p. 30, "Unanswered *Science* Questions."

A Potpourri of Blessings

Hebrews 6:7

"For the earth which drinketh in the rain that cometh oft upon it, and bringeth forth herbs meet for them by whom it is dressed, receiveth blessing from God...."

Many people like to have a nice perfume around the house. They brew a potpourri of mint, citronella, lavender and similar fragrant plants to make home smell more like home. But humans aren't the only creatures that appreciate a nice smell around their house.

During field studies scientists have found that a small bird called the Corsican Blue Tit also like to have a pleasant-smelling nest. This was an unexpected discovery, made quite accidentally when one researcher discovered various sprigs of aromatic plants in dozens of nests. When she starts to lay her eggs, the female bird will begin keeping her nest stocked with fresh, fragrant herbs until all the eggs hatch. The birds prefer yarrow, citronella, mint and lavender. When researchers secretly removed these herbs from the nests that they were observing, the parent birds were quick to replace the fragrant sprigs with others. It also turns out that these herbs also have disinfectant and anti-pest characteristics. They inhibit bacteria and fungi and act as mosquito repellents. Rather than simply beautifying their nests or adding a nice perfume, the birds are also protecting their offspring from diseases and pests. You might wonder, Who taught them to do this?

As the Bible says, herbs are a blessing from God. They are not just a blessing to man, but also to many of God's creatures.

Prayer: Lord, I thank You for all of the blessings You have given us. I especially thank You that You sent Your Son to save us. Amen.

Ref: *Discover*, 11/02, p. 13, Josie Glausiusz, "Eau D'Oiseau."

The Secrets of Hot Mineral Water

Genesis 7:11b

"... the same day were all the fountains of the great deep broken up, and the windows of heaven were opened."

How long does it take for large mineral formations to form? While evolutionists say millions of years, creationists assume that most of the rock formations we see formed relatively quickly as the waters of the Genesis flood receded.

In 1903, someone pounded an iron pipe into the ground in what is today, Hot Springs State Park. The mineral-rich water beneath the ground immediately began flowing out of the pipe. As the warm mineral water evaporated, the minerals that were left behind, deposited as travertine. Within just a few years, there was a mound of travertine as high as the pipe and tapering to the ground. Today, the water has stopped flowing. What remains today is a mound of minerals sheeted in pastel curtains over 20 feet high and more than 15 feet across.

The Bible's description of the fountains of the deep being broken up at the beginning of the Genesis flood suggests huge hot water geysers. Much of that water would undoubtedly have been like the mineral-rich waters of today's hot springs. This mineral water then mixed with the sediment created by the violence of the flood. As the sediment finally settled out and the waters dried up, the remaining minerals would help quickly bind the sediment together into the sedimentary rock layers we commonly see today. Those long evolutionary ages would be unnecessary.

Prayer: Father, I thank You that in Christ, you do not judge me as You judged those in Noah's day. Amen.

Ref: *Creation*, 9-11/05, p. 56, Tas Walker, "A Monstrous Mound of ... Minerals!"

The Latest on What Plants Are Saying

Psalm 33:20

"Our soul waiteth for the LORD: he is our help and our shield."

In past ***Creation Moments*** we have told how certain plants release aromatics known as pheromones when attacked. By this means they communicate to others of its species or even to animals. These discoveries led more researchers to enter this field and a great deal is now known about what can only be called plant communication.

Researchers report that this plant communication is more widespread than thought, in fact, they suspect that it is almost universal among plants. What's more, plants not only communicate with their own species, but with other plants and even with animals. Some, like the wild tobacco, even know not to communicate when the intended recipient of the message is not around. It does not emit its anti-caterpillar scent until night time when nocturnal moths are liable to be around to lay eggs on them. Should the moths lay eggs on the plants the plant will signal to an all-purpose insect ally to eat the eggs. That same ally will also eat other insect pests that harm the plant. Scientists say that not only are the plants' messages specific, it appears that an individual plant will vary its message based on its experience.

That plants even communicate with other species is a wonder that cannot be explained by chance mutations. That their messages are so specific bespeaks the intelligence of their Creator.

Prayer: Father, I thank You that I can call out to You when I need help and You will help me because I am Yours in Christ. Amen.

Ref: *Discover*, 4/02, pp. 46-51, Sharman Apt Russel, "Talking Plants."

True Superglue

Psalm 9:1

"I will praise thee, O LORD, with my whole heart; I will shew forth all thy marvellous works."

Try using superglue in wet conditions and you'll find that the glue is not so super. Even epoxy doesn't work well in water. Scientists finally decided to turn to the lowly mussel to learn how to make better glues for use in wet environments.

Mussels manufacture their glue under water, yet the glue can withstand the force of thousand pounds per square inch. Mussel glue will even stick to Teflon! The mussel begins by making the glue in two parts, each part of the glue is made by a separate gland. One gland produces proteins that are like resin. The other gland makes the hardeners. When these are mixed, they harden into a strand in only a couple of minutes. The mussel will make many of these strands as it fastens itself to a rock. As more of these strands are made, they begin to cross-link with one another, greatly adding to the strength of the bond. The mussel makes between five and ten different kinds of protein strands, carefully limiting the cross-linking to produce the greatest strength. Without this mix, the bond would be brittle and easily break.

God's creation is marvelously designed. His designs are still teaching us how to do even simple things better. The theory of evolution depends upon random chance events that even if believable can teach us nothing.

Prayer: Father, I stand in awe of Your handiwork and rejoice in Your salvation. Amen.

Ref: *Discover*, 2/03, pp. 22-23, Alan Burdick, "Cement on the Half Shell."

The Biggest Flower You Wouldn't Want

Song of Solomon 2:12

"The flowers appear on the earth; the time of the singing of birds is come, and the voice of the turtle is heard in our land...."

The largest flower in the world is a bright red-orange color and, according to its DNA, is related to the poinsettia. That relationship might make you suspect that world's largest flower would be beautiful. But you probably wouldn't want the flower, called the rafflesia, growing in your garden.

The largest of this species has flower buds the size of a basketball. When it opens, the flower is three feet across. Its petals not only look like big slabs of meat but the flower smells like rotting meat. The result is a rather ugly flower that you wouldn't want around. That bad smell attracts the carrion-eating insects that pollinate it. The flower looks so strange that when they were first discovered, scientists debated whether they were flowering plants or fungi. If this is not all strange enough, rafflesias have no true roots or leaves. They make their living as parasites growing on other plants. This makes them so difficult to grow that only four botanical gardens in the world have done it successfully.

The rafflesia's beauty lies not in its appearance, but in its amazing design features. Little about its design seems to be helpful for survival, as evidenced by how difficult it is to grow. This fact, of course, works against evolution's claim that the living things we see are the survivors of the fittest.

Prayer: Father, I praise Your unlimited creativity and the care You provide to all of Your creatures. Amen.

Ref: *Science News*, 1/13/07, p. 21, S. Milius, "Biggest Bloom."

Monkeys as Intelligent as College Students?

Colossians 4:6

"Let your speech be alway with grace, seasoned with salt, that ye may know how ye ought to answer every man."

Evolutionists claim that human intelligence began to develop when early man invented language. Genesis tells us that human language began when Adam named the animals. Names, that is, nouns are the first requirement for language but this must be preceded by intelligence. Creationists have always viewed both language and intelligence as gifts from God.

New research disproves the old evolutionary idea. Of course, we use language to test human intelligence using, say, a series of cards. Researchers at Columbia University did something similar with rhesus macaques. They sat the monkeys in front of computers with touch screens. The screens showed seven photographs that were not in sequential order. After learning how to place the photographs in order, the monkeys did just that for a banana pellet. This task involves both memory and logic. The monkeys quickly became good at ordering the photos. As they were shown new pictures they showed that they could apply what they had learned to new problems. What's more, they learned the task as quickly as a control group made up of college students!

Since the monkeys in this experiment don't use language, and they clearly possess memory and logic, language cannot be the source of our intelligence. A better explanation is that both language and intelligence are the gifts of God, given us by the Word Who created us.

Prayer: Father, thank You for the gifts of language and intelligence. Help me to always use these gifts to Your glory. Amen.

Ref: *Discover*, 6/03, p. 13, Jocelyn Selim, "The Smart, Speechless Types."

True Milk of Human Kindness

Jeremiah 32:22

"And hast given them this land, which thou didst swear to their fathers to give them, a land flowing with milk and honey...."

While many people recognize the virtues of feeding their infants human breast milk, science is still learning its amazing secrets. Although cow's milk contains many substances found in human milk, it does not contain certain very specific substances necessary to protect the infant.

Human milk not only helps protect the infant's digestive system by discouraging bad bacteria, it also introduces and encourages good bacteria. In fact, some of the good bacteria that protect the infant are found in no other place on earth. Oligosaccharides in milk kill bad bacteria in a way in which the bad bacteria can never develop immunity. Lactoferrin in human milk can suppress inflammation. It also boosts the immune system and kills viruses, bad bacteria and fungi. Not only does the mother's milk pass mom's immunities on to the infant, the milk's oligosaccharides give infants immunity to germs the mother has never even encountered. The protein alphalactalbumin, in an acid environment such as the digestive tract, can even reduce warts and kills cancer cells. So far, alphalactalbumin has been shown to effectively kill forty different kinds of cancer cells. Use of this protein in preliminary clinical trials to treat bladder cancer has been promising.

God has given us so many good things, we are still only discovering them. But the greatest of His gifts is salvation through His Son, Jesus Christ.

Prayer: Dear Father, thank You for all Your good gifts, especially the forgiveness of sins, eternal life and salvation. Amen.

Ref: *Science News*, 12/9/06, pp. 376-378, Julie J. Rehmeyer, "Milk Therapy."

The Sounds Smells Right

Psalm 4:1

"Hear me when I call, O God of my righteousness: thou hast enlarged me when I was in distress; have mercy upon me, and hear my prayer."

Insects offer some novel designs. For example, they can have ears on their stomachs, wings or legs. Now scientists at the University of Zurich in Switzerland have discovered an even more novel arrangement in the fruit fly.

Scientists have been aware for many years that fruit flies can respond to sound. Sound plays an important part in their mating rituals. However, scientists were unsure just how the fruit fly's hearing worked. They also knew that their antennae, known singularly as arista, had something to do with the way the fruit fly can hear sound. Because an arista is so small, only 300 microns long, scientists have until recently, lacked the ability to take the fine measurements necessary to find out what is really going on. Now all that has been overcome and we learn that the base of the arista, which also senses smells, actually turns each arista toward the incoming sound. In short, the fruit fly actually rotates its nose so that it can hear better. Researchers have since found a similar arrangement in related flies. They suspect that such an arrangement will be found in several related species.

As amazing as this arrangement is, God's greatest wisdom is seen in His plan of salvation. Through His Son, Jesus Christ, He has gained the victory of sin, death and Satan for mankind.

Prayer: I praise You, heavenly Father, as I see Your wisdom all around me, especially in Your plan of salvation for me. Amen.

Ref: *Science News*, 6/23/01, p. 391, S. Milius, "Fruit Flies Hear by Spinning Their Noses."

Singing Mice?

Psalm 40:3

"And he hath put a new song in my mouth, even praise unto our God: many shall see it, and fear, and shall trust in the LORD."

Birds do it. Whales do it. Now, it appears that male mice do it. They all sing!

Scientists have long known that mice produce ultrasound. Their pitch is about two octaves above what we can hear. For example, when mouse pups lose track of mom they begin to cry so that mom can find them. Researchers carried out investigations to see whether there is any structure to the sounds that adult mice make. They did this by recording the vocalizations of 45 male mice. Then they slowed down the recordings to study them. The researchers found distinct syllables at about ten syllables per second. In addition, their "voices" also rise and fall in pitch at varying rates. The research then found that certain syllables were repeated, creating phrasing sequences that sound very much like music. The researchers compare the mouse vocalizations to the songs sung by whales and birds. While other scientists recognize that the mouse sounds are not random, they question whether they should be called "song".

We know that music is a gift from God. It appears that God has been generous with His gift of music, and just possibly has even extended this to the animal kingdom. However, only we humans have the privilege of praising Him with words and music for His gift of salvation through His Son, Jesus Christ.

Prayer: I praise You, Father, for the gift and beauty of music and for sharing it with so much of Your creation. Amen.

Ref: *Science News*, 11/5/05, p. 293, B. Harder "Beyond Falsetto."

A Most Amazing Escape Artist

Job 38:41

"Who provideth for the raven his food? when his young ones cry unto God, they wander for lack of meat."

A parasitic worm that matures on land, but must breed under the water has some remarkable abilities to make this difficult trick possible.

The worm grows to maturity on dry land, but must return to a body of water to find a mate and breed. It grows inside insects like crickets. The insects it infests are typically not aquatic, making this problem number one. When breeding time comes, the worm causes the insect to move in such an uncontrolled manner that it eventually ends up in the water. Once in the water, it takes the worm about 10 minutes to escape from the insect. However, an insect struggling on the surface of the water is very attractive to a hungry fish. This is problem number two. But if the worm can't wriggle free of the insect before it is eaten, the worm has more abilities to put into play. The worm inside an eaten insect continues to wriggle until it finally escapes through the fish's mouth or gills. Scientists studying the worm reported observing six escapes each from frogs and perch and more than 20 escapes from trout.

God has marvelously provided for this little worm. But then, this is easy for Him, considering He has provided us with escape from sin, death and Satan through the innocent death of His Son, Jesus Christ.

Prayer: Thank You for providing for all Your creatures, Father, and especially for providing me salvation in Jesus Christ. Amen.

Ref: *Science News*, 4/22/06, p. 252, "Worm Can Crawl Out of Predator."

The Lazarus Rat

1 Corinthians 8:2

"And if any man think that he knoweth any thing, he knoweth nothing yet as he ought to know."

According to evolutionists, the early family of mammals called Diatomyidae, has been extinct for eleven million years. Of course, as creationists, we do not accept this dating. This Diatomyidae family included rat-like creatures with long skulls, a furry tail and rounded ears.

Then, in 1996, a wildlife-survey team bought some strange looking animals in a meat market in Laos. This led to the discovery of living Laotian rock rats. These animals were placed into a family that includes porcupines and guinea pigs. Others argued that it belonged to a new family. The debate sparked a more detailed look at its DNA and bone structure by researchers in five countries. The results ruled out any possibility that the rats were related to guinea pigs. But the rock rat's characteristic long skull, furred tail and round ears seem to settle the matter. The Diatomyidae are not extinct and the Laotian rock rat is indeed a member of this family. This discovery of thought-to-be extinct families happens frequently enough that such families are called Lazarus taxon or, more popularly, "living fossils."

So, when evolutionists proclaim that this or that creature or family has been extinct for millions of years, it takes only one living specimen to disprove it. Furthermore, many creatures do not appear in the recent fossil record and this puts the entire interpretation into question.

Prayer: Lord, I yield all my wisdom to Your greater wisdom, and ask for Your Holy Spirit to grant me heavenly wisdom. Amen.

Ref: *Science News*, 4/28/07, p. 260, S. Milius, "Living Fossil."

Fish Birth Amazes Evolutionists

Job 12:8

"Or speak to the earth, and it shall teach thee: and the fishes of the sea shall declare unto thee."

It was nice day on a tropical reef in what is now Western Australia when an armored fish began to give birth. Before she could finish, the violence of the Genesis Flood encased her in mud.

Of course, that's not how evolutionists interpret the evidence. Our mom-to-be is a member of a newly discovered species of placoderm, a family of now-extinct armored fish. Not only were these fish armored, their jaws could apparently crush bones. Evolutionists say that these fish lived between 354 and 417 million inflated evolutionary years ago. This discovery pushes back the first-known example of a fish giving live birth 200 million evolutionary years ago. After the discovery, scientists went back and studied the fossils of another placoderm and discovered that it, too, had a uterus with three apparent unborn pups in it. Scientists say that the partially born youngster was already a quarter of its mother's ten-inch length. This helped its survival in a fish-eat-fish world. Scientists admit that the fish had an unexpectedly sophisticated reproductive system. Such systems, they say, are found only in supposedly much more evolved fish.

Of course, like all other living things, the placoderms did not evolve but were created. Their so-called advanced reproductive system does not show evidence for evolutionary progression, but it *does* show evidence of a caring Creator.

Prayer: Lord, the entire creation declares the excellence of Your handiwork. Help me to do so, too. Amen.

Ref: http:www.livescience.com/animals/080528-fossil-embryo.html

Security Mites

Psalm 20:1

"The LORD hear thee in the day of trouble; the name of the God of Jacob defend thee...."

The potter wasp is a solitary wasp that makes a mud nest with several rooms in it. At egg-laying time, the wasp lays one egg in each cavity and leaves some food in each cavity. She also leaves behind a security force!

You see, there is another species of parasitic wasp that seeks out a potter wasp nest to lay its eggs. When it is successful, the baby potter wasps would have no chance of survival if it wasn't for the security force. The mother potter wasp has very specialized pockets on its back. Tiny mites live within those pockets, causing no harm to the wasp. Then, while the potter wasp lays her eggs, some of the mites exit and remain in each room with the egg. These mites will remain in the nest after it is sealed, feeding on the food left for the hatchlings. They also mate at this time, which conveniently provides a population of mites as food for the young potter wasps. While these mites are peaceful creatures, they are the security force, and should a parasitic wasp get into the nest, they eagerly attack it.

This arrangement that benefits both the potter wasp and the mites is too intricate to have come about by accident. It was designed by the same Creator Who protects His children.

Prayer: Thank You, Father, for Your care and protection, especially Your protection from the devil through Christ's victory. Amen.

Ref: http://www.sciencenews.org/view/generic/id/33774/title/Mighty_mites

Homer May Have Been Smarter than We Thought

Psalm 147:4

"He telleth the number of the stars; he calleth them all by their names."

Homer, the blind Greek poet, spoke of Odysseus's return to Ithaca and describes some astronomical events that seldom happen in the order he describes. Yet, the setting of the events he writes about took place 400 years before it is thought Homer lived.

As Odysseus sails home five days before a banquet, he notes that both the constellations Boötes and Pleia des are visible. Because of their placement in the sky, they are very rarely visible in the same sky in Greece. Homer also mentions Odysseus's sighting of Venus just before dawn. Then, on the day of the banquet there is a solar eclipse. Some have dismissed these details as just colorful descriptions in a fictional poem. However, a solar eclipse did take place in that part of the world on April 16, 1178 B.C., just the time period Homer is writing about. Researchers then figured out the positions of the other astronomical features Odysseus is reported to have seen, and they were indeed happening on and within days of that date as described. The problem is, Greek astronomy at Homer's time was not believed to be sophisticated enough to figure out where these astronomical bodies were 400 years earlier.

Perhaps man, who has made astronomical observatories since before most historic cultures were established, was originally given such knowledge by his Creator.

Prayer: Father, I thank You for the beauty of the night sky that so gloriously sets forth Your glory and power. Amen.

Ref: http://www.sciencenews.org/view/generic/id/33683/title/Too_much_information_in_the_Odyssey

A Serpent Can Point to Christ

John 3:14

"And as Moses lifted up the serpent in the wilderness, even so must the Son of man be lifted up...."

The Tiger Keelback snake has a bite that delivers slow-acting venom and prevents the victim's blood from clotting. An adult human could bleed to death from a bite, but it takes a while for the snake to deliver a lethal dose.

When threatened, the average Keelback will raise its head and display its colorful swollen neck. Should the attacker bite the snake near its head, it will get a mouth full of a much stronger poison from glands in its neck. Where does that poison come from? For years scientists have debated whether the Keelback produces its own poison, or does it get the poison from some other creature that it ate? Now research has revealed that the Keelback actually does store the poison of a poisonous toad that it eats. Moreover, it seems to know that it has this poison stored. For example, on an island where there are some Keelbacks but no toads, these Keelbacks when threatened do not display their neck to an attacker. Rather, they flee from their attacker.

God has used many ingenious designs in His creation, knowing that some would recognize this and, by doing so, acknowledge His existence, power and glory. His desire is always that we might be driven to His Word to learn of the salvation He has prepared for us in Jesus Christ.

Prayer: Father, I thank You that You desire our salvation and that You have called me to faith in Jesus Christ. Amen.

Ref: *Science News*, 2/3/07, p. 69, S. Milius, "Bite This."

Delicate Beauty

Revelation 21:4

"And God shall wipe away all tears from their eyes; and there shall be no more death, neither sorrow, nor crying, neither shall there be any more pain: for the former things are passed away."

Bacteria and fungi form biofilms on just about every wet surface, like that bowl of water you left out last night! In this biofilm state, bacteria cause 70 percent of all human bacterial infections. On underwater pipelines, biofilms cause corrosion. Such biofilms even form on seaweed. That is, except for the seaweed called Delicate Beauty.

Delicate Beauty, grows off the coast of Australia, and researchers long wondered why biofilms never form on this seaweed. Researchers have now discovered that Delicate Beauty secretes chemicals called furanones. Furanones don't kill the bacteria, but prevent it from colonizing by repelling them. This observation is important because it is believed that since the furanones don't kill the bacteria, the bacteria will not develop a resistance to the furanones. Commercial production of these chemicals are now beginning to be used in water-cooling towers to prevent biofilm buildup and in clinical trials on contact lenses to prevent bacterial growth. So far these trials have been successful, and further applications are under study.

It was not God's desire that disease and death should come into His creation because of our sin. But He knew that it would. So He stocked the creation with things for us to discover to alleviate and avoid some of our suffering in this world. Christians know that there is no disease or death in heaven.

Prayer: Father, while we will experience no disease when we get to heaven, I thank You for giving us tools to prevent it here. Amen.

Ref: *Science Illustrated*, 7-8/08, pp. 62-69, "Inspired by Nature."

No Eyes, But It Can See Light

Psalm 94:9

"He that planted the ear, shall he not hear? He that formed the eye, shall he not see?"

It turns out that not all creatures need eyes to see light. It all depends on what the creatures were designed to do. The roundworm, *C. elegans*, lives below the soil surface where it needs no eyes. At the same time, this roundworm needs to sense light because too much exposure will kill it. Researchers noted that the roundworm has only 302 nerve cells. Study of these cells showed that some of them sense light in the same way that similar cells in vertebrates sense light. Evolutionists suggested that this is an example of an early step in the evolution of eyes. However, there is no evolutionary pressure for this roundworm to evolve eyes, because light will kill it. Besides, animals that supposedly evolved long before *C. elegans* already had eyes. A better explanation is that, like the cave fishes, this roundworm lives in the dark and needs no eyes and would, in any case, be constantly filling with dirt. No, this is not an example of evolution, but of good design by God.

God has designed all things to fit well into their respective environments. The fish that lives in the dark depths of the ocean and has lighted lures, the fishes that live in the darkest caves have no eyes and neither does the roundworm, *C. elegans*. All these show God's fingerprints.

Prayer: Father, You have made all things well, showing Your wisdom and power for all to see. Thank You. Amen.

Ref: http://www.sciencenews.org/view/generic/id/33889/title/Seeing_without_eyes

Smart Slime

Ecclesiastes 4:9

"Two are better than one; because they have a good reward for their labour."

We all know that there is strength in numbers. Many animals have even discovered this and, for example, migrate in large herds. However, one would never expect bacteria to have discovered this or know enough to organize themselves collectively.

Bacteria consist of a single cell that doesn't even have a nucleus. They have no nervous system, and they reproduce by simply dividing in half. Of course, there is no brain; yet, they seem to display a sense of consciousness that totally baffles the neurosciences. Some marine species of bacteria are able to sense when there are other bacteria around them. Then, when a sufficient number have gathered together, their metabolism changes, and they begin to produce a slime that then holds them together. While all this is now known, new research shows that the slime, called biofilm, includes chemicals that are poisonous to the very predators that would ordinarily feed on the bacteria. In fact, the biofilm seems to protect the bacteria. The more bacteria there are, the more biofilm they make and the more protection they have from predators.

There are no simple forms of life. Even bacteria, which are an important part of the ecosystem, have been designed with the ability to protect themselves – something they could never have invented for themselves.

Prayer: Father, while You teach us to help one another, help me to always look to Your strength for my aid. Amen.

Ref: *Minneapolis Star Tribune*, 7/29/08, p. A5, David Brown, "Cellmates: Research shows that bacteria, when under attack, stick together to survive."

Are "Cavemen" Primitive?

1 Kings 19:9

"And he came thither unto a cave, and lodged there; and, behold, the word of the LORD came to him...."

Cavemen. The very word conjures images of bear skin clothing, wooden clubs and perhaps some simple stone tools. We think of the cavemen themselves as part ape and certainly less than modern humans. All of these images help make human evolution look more plausible.

However, in China there are some 20 million people living in caves. The caves there are easily carved in the silty soil of the Western regions of the Yellow River. The caves are generally 10 to 13 feet wide and can extend as far as 25 feet back into the hillside. Sometimes the caves are connected to one another, creating a larger place to live. Many of the people who live in these caves would not think of moving out of them. Caves are warm in the winter, cool in the summer, and they are fireproof. These caves include flues for venting the exhaust from cooking fires. But these caves are not primitive dwellings by any stretch of the imagination. They feature plumbing, electrical wiring and even cable television! Except for windows, some of these cave homes are as modern as anything you'll see in the rest of the developing world.

Throughout the ages, people have taken shelter in caves and even set up housekeeping in them. The fact that they lived in caves does not make them primitive at all.

Prayer: Lord, do not let Your people be misled into unbelief, and enlighten them with Your truth. Amen.

Ref: *Minneapolis Star Tribune*, 12/21/08, p. AA5, Tim Johnson, "Cave, sweet cave: Many Chinese find home is in a hillside."

Australia's Smart Dolphins

Psalm 104:27

"These wait all upon thee; that thou mayest give them their meat in due season."

It was once thought that only man used tools. However, scientists have learned that some monkeys and even some birds use "tools." Now we can add dolphins to the growing list of tool-users.

Researchers studying dolphins in Australia's Shark Bay noticed that some dolphins were swimming around with sponges on their beaks. After some observation, both on the surface and beneath the water, scientists discovered what the dolphins were doing. Holding the sponges in their mouths, they would sweep the sea bottom sand, flushing out fish. Then they dropped the sponge and ate what they had flushed out. When they were finished eating, they retrieved their sponge and repeated the process. Researchers found that about 10 percent of the females obtained their food using sponges as tools. For some unknown reason, very few of the males used this method. Furthermore, most of the females using this method were related to two maternal tool-using dolphins. Researchers debate whether these two taught their descendants this method of obtaining fish or whether the behavior is based in genetics.

Since this is not a widespread behavior among dolphins, it seems likely that it is a learned behavior probably taught to younger relatives by the maternal dolphins. After all, dolphins are known to be very intelligent, and intelligence is a gift from their Creator.

Prayer: I thank You, Lord, that You have given Your creatures an Earth and the ability to make a living on it. Amen.

Ref: Science News Online, 12/10/08, www.sciencenews.org/view/generic/id/39219, Bruce Bower, "Dolphins Wield Tools of the Sea."

Three-Dimensional Thinking

Matthew 22:37

"Jesus said unto him, Thou shalt love the Lord thy God with all thy heart, and with all thy soul, and with all thy mind."

Without a doubt the brain is a marvelous organ, although there is still a great deal to learn about how it works. We do know that brain cells communicate through connections which reach out in three dimensions to other cells. When thought and motion take place, they communicate with each other very quickly. They are even in communication while you sleep.

In contrast to the human brain, the "thinking" parts of a computer are connected in two dimensions to "communicate" with each other. Researchers thought that it might boost performance if a three-dimensional computer chip could be designed. Cell phones already use a three-dimensional chip arrangement, but these are just individual flat chips stacked one on top of another. Researchers wanted to see what true three-dimensional chips (called TSVs), could do. Now several chip manufacturers have developed working TSVs. They have found that three-dimensional chips transmit information faster and use less power than flat chips. In other words, they are more efficient than flat chips and pack more "thinking" power into a smaller space. Chip manufacturers are now working on ways to successfully mass produce the TSVs.

The three-dimensional computer chip does improve chip performance by mimicking the wiring of the brain. However, except in the area of calculation, we are nowhere close to mimicking the power of the human brain.

Prayer: Thank You, Father, for implanting in my mind faith in Jesus Christ as my Lord and Savior. Amen.

Ref: *The Nikkei Weekly*, 12/29/08 & 1/5/09, p. 3, "Semiconductor makers head for third dimension."

Great Travelers Have Great Stories to Tell

Acts 11:19a

"Now they which were scattered abroad upon the persecution that arose about Stephen traveled as far as Phoenicia, and Cyprus, and Antioch...."

Those who widely travel usually have interesting experiences to talk about. That is no less true of animals that migrate. A commonly known example is the monarch butterfly. In the fall, monarchs from all over North America head south to the same small patch of jungle trees in Mexico. Even more astonishing is that each generation finds this exact traditional wintering spot but has never been there before.

Scientists have recently discovered that another migrating creature has an even more interesting story to tell. Bar-tailed godwits, shorebirds with a wingspan of about 12 to 16 inches, summer in Alaska. But they winter in New Zealand, over 7,000 miles away. As you mentally picture their route, you would be right to notice that there are very few places to stop and rest between Alaska and New Zealand. Researchers outfitted seven female godwits with tracking devices to learn more about their migration. They found that the godwits traveled the distance nonstop, without rest or even food or water. That's the equivalent of a nonstop flight from London to Los Angeles, plus 1,000 miles more!

Godwits glorify God as Creator with their amazing migratory paths. As the first Christians scattered across the Roman Empire in fear of persecution and martyrdom, they spread the wonder of God's love for us in the Gospel of salvation.

Prayer: Father, I thank You for the glory of Your creation, but I rejoice in the wonder of Your love and salvation. Amen.

Ref: *Science News*, 11/22/08, p. 14, Laura Sanders, "Nonstop godwit flights."

Stressed Plants Tell Us About It

Ezekiel 47:12b

"...and the fruit thereof shall be for meat, and the leaf thereof for medicine."

When they have a headache or perhaps a toothache many people take an aspirin. It turns out that many plants do almost the same thing when they are under stress.

The plants that do so, however, make their own form of aspirin called methyl salicylate. This phenomenon has been observed in the laboratory, but never in nature until now. Researchers studying air pollution set up their instruments near a California walnut grove. They wanted to see what gases the plants might be emitting. Methyl salicylate was among the gases they detected. Researchers believe that the gas might have some immune function for the plants. It might also warn surrounding plants of a threat. This finding may help farmers and others detect when plants are being stressed by lack of water, insects or disease. Until this finding, those caring for plants could only tell when a plant was stressed once the plant began to show visible signs of stress. With this information, those who tend plants will be able to apply pesticides, for example, in a more timely manner.

God gave us a perfect world where there was no need for medicines. But He knew we would sin and bring death and sickness upon the creation. So, being a loving God, He also gave us medicines to discover and ease our suffering.

Prayer: Thank You, Father, for the gift of medicine. Prosper all good knowledge that brings healing in our midst. Amen.

Ref: *Yahoo! News*, 9/18/08, Randolf E. Schmid, AP Science Writer, "Stressed plants produce aspirin-like chemical."

Dolphins at Play

Job 40:20

"Surely the mountains bring him forth food, where all the beasts of the field play."

Bottlenose dolphins have a reputation as intelligent, playful creatures. A newly released video shows just how intelligent their play is.

The video shows various dolphins creating rotating bubble rings which seem to hover in the water for a few seconds. The dolphins do this by first creating a water vortex with their dorsal fin. The ends of the vortex then come together into an invisible ring. Then the dolphin injects air from its blowhole into the spinning vortex. The vortex has enough energy to hold the ring from rising too quickly for play. Such a vortex bubble is about two feet across. However, dolphins might play with the vortex to create a smaller ring. Sometimes a dolphin will insert a smaller bubble ring inside a larger ring. They also create rings that flip vertically or even flip completely over. Sometimes a dolphin will create two bubble rings that collide and produce a third ring. The video shows one dolphin creating a large ring and watching it rise through the water. Just before the ring breaks the surface, the dolphin swims through the ring and leaps from the water.

Intelligence and such play as this are linked. Our Creator has not just shared intelligence and creativity with man. He clearly has shared some of His intelligence and creativity with His other creatures as well.

Prayer: Father, thank You for the beauty of Your creation and sharing Your creativity with so much of Your creation. Amen.

Ref: http://www.snopes.com/photos/animals/dolphinrings.asp, "Video shows dolphins creating and playing with bubble rings."

Antibiotic Resistant No More

Genesis 22:8

"And Abraham said, My son, God will provide himself a lamb for a burnt offering: so they went both of them together."

One of medicine's greatest challenges are those populations of bacteria that have become resistant to antibiotics.

The ocean is literally a soup of bio-germs, including bacteria, many of which can infect, sicken and kill a wide variety of creatures. These germs often form biofilms which protect them from antibiotics. Marine researchers were investigating the ocean bottom where something had killed all the marine creatures. In the midst of all this death they found a thriving marine sponge. Why wasn't it dead like everything else? Studying the sponge's defenses, researchers discovered a chemical called ageliferin. Further study showed that this compound prevented biofilms from forming. What's more, the chemical makes resistant germs once again susceptible to antibiotics. It has already been proven to re-sensitize bacteria that cause ear infections, food poisoning, whooping cough and a particularly nasty resistant bacteria that causes infections in hospitals.

While God gave us a perfect world, He knew that mankind would sin and bring disease and death into the world. So God provided antibiotics. But He also knew that some germs would become resistant to antibiotics. So He provided His creation with substances to solve that problem, too. Nevertheless, mankind's primary problem is sin, and He provided us with the Lamb of God Who takes away the sin of the world – one repentant sinner at a time.

Prayer: I thank You, Lord, for good medicine, but most of all I thank You for sending Your Son to be my Savior. Amen.

Ref: *Science News*, 3/14/09, p. 16, Laura Sanders, "Sponge's secret weapon revealed."

Evolutionary Model of Early Earth's Atmosphere Fails Test

Genesis 1:31

"And God saw every thing that he had made, and, behold, it was very good. And the evening and the morning were the sixth day."

According to the theory of evolution, the atmosphere of the very early Earth contained no oxygen, but it did contain carbon dioxide. When the plants and trees evolved, they lived on the carbon-dioxide as they still do today and, by metabolizing carbon dioxide, they released oxygen as a waste product.

When sufficient oxygen had been produced, air-breathing animals evolved, but this was supposedly a slow process. Calculations showed that by the time the dinosaurs were beginning to die out, 65 million evolutionary years ago, the Earth's atmosphere only contained 10 to 12 percent oxygen. Today, the atmosphere is 21 percent oxygen. But to complicate the issue, there is much fossil evidence of wildfires during this era. The researchers wondered whether the small amount of oxygen that was supposedly in the atmosphere then could support such fires under realistic conditions. Tests were carried out in an atmosphere containing 12 percent oxygen using paper, matches, wooden sticks and a candle. The results showed that none of these items will burn readily until the atmosphere contains a minimum of 17 percent oxygen. The evolutionary model of the early Earth's atmosphere was proven wrong!

When God finished creating, He declared that everything was "very good." That includes the design of the atmosphere with enough oxygen to support life, but not too much to cause fire to burn explosively.

Prayer: Father, thank You for so wisely designing the Earth's atmosphere so that it supports life. Amen.

Ref: *Science*, 29 August 2008, pp. 1197-1200, C.M. Belcher, J.C. McElwain, "Limits for Combustion in Low Co_2 Redefine Paleoatmospheric Predictions for the Mesozoic."

Designed as a Companion

Genesis 9:2a

"And the fear of you and the dread of you shall be upon every beast of the earth, and upon every fowl of the air...."

When God told Noah that man could now eat meat after the Flood, He kindly filled the animals with a natural fear of man. However, He evidently left a few animals without that fear in order for them to be helpmates and companions for man.

The dog has been man's best friend probably since before the Genesis Flood. Researchers recently tested whether Border Collies were intelligent enough to fetch an unseen item in another room simply by being shown a picture or model of it. Chimps and dolphins had also been tested for this ability and were unable to do it. Collies, both trained and untrained to "fetch", were tested in their own homes. Eight toys they were to fetch were in a second room. Then the dogs were shown either an exact copy of what they were to fetch, a model of it, or a photograph and were told, "bring it here." All retrieved their toy easily after being shown a model of it. Trained dogs did well when shown an exact copy, but the untrained dogs needed a little practice with this task. Some dogs were even able to fetch a toy when shown a full-sized photograph.

Not only does the domestic dog have no natural fear of man, but many of them can relate to us in very helpful ways.

Prayer: Father, thank You for those animals which can be companions and even help us. Amen.

Ref: *Science News* Online, 3/21/09, http://www.sciencenews.org/view/generic/id/419732, Bruce Bower, "Dogs Show a Fetching Communication Savvy."

Salad Spiders

Genesis 1:30

"And to every beast of the earth, and to every fowl of the air... I have given every green herb for meat: and it was so."

In the perfect world that God created there were no meat eaters. In today's sinful world it is hard to imagine meat eaters, like spiders, being vegetarians.

Some spiders have occasionally been observed tasting plants. The male crab spider has been seen tasting plant nectar. Some baby spiders eat spores that they find in their webs. But now a small jumping spider that lives on acacia trees has been discovered that is vegetarian. Acacia trees are often home to vicious ants that protect the tree from other gnawing insects. In return, the tree offers the ants protection and tasty nectar. So the little jumping spider must constantly avoid the guard ants when it heads out for a meal of nectar. One of their strategies for avoiding ants is to build their nests on mature leaves. These leaves are the least guarded on the plant. Researchers noted that they did observe four instances of a spider eating ant larva, but this was out of 140 feeding observations.

Our experiences in a fallen world do not begin to prepare us for what God is able to create, despite all the wonders around us. If it pleases God, He can make vegetarian lions, tigers and even spiders. Who of us would ever have thought of His plan to rescue us from sin through His Son, Jesus Christ?

Prayer: Thank You, dear Father, for providing for all of Your creatures, even in a fallen world. Amen.

Ref: *Science News* online, http://www.sciencenews.org/view/generic/id/35121, 8/12/08, Susan Milius, "Vegetarian Spider."

The Lotus Effect

1 John 1:9

"If we confess our sins, he is faithful and just to forgive us our sins, and to cleanse us from all unrighteousness."

Perhaps you have a self-cleaning oven in your kitchen, and if you have small children in your house, you've probably wished for self-cleaning walls. Self-cleaning clothes would be nice, too!

Lotuses often grow in muddy water where mud can accumulate on leaves. Yet, for efficiency in collecting sunlight, their leaves need to be clean. And, yes, they stay clean despite the environment in which they grow. Close examination under a powerful electron microscope reveals why. The top of the leaves are covered with tiny spikes that feel waxy. They are so tiny that they can even hold up a particle of dust that settles on a leaf. As a result, any water that lands on the leaves rolls right off. As it rolls off, it collects any dirt that may be on a leaf. These leaves are self-cleaning! Researchers realized that this microscopic spike structure could be used to make self- cleaning products. For example, self-cleaning paint for homes is already in use under the product name Lotusan. Self-cleaning food containers are being developed as well. And one day we may even have self-cleaning clothes, including swimming suits that never get wet.

However, when it comes to our standing before God, we are not self-cleaning. We must rely on the cleansing from our sin won for us by our Lord Jesus on the cross.

Prayer: Father, thank You for the forgiveness of sins I have through my Lord Jesus Christ and the life He gives me. Amen.

Ref: *Science Illustrated*, 7/8/08, pp. 62-69, "Inspired by Nature," ("Mr. Clean," pp. 68-69).

"God Bless You" Indeed

Matthew 6:26

"Behold the fowls of the air: for they sow not, neither do they reap, nor gather into barns; yet your heavenly Father feedeth them."

Most people know that if they are stranded at sea without fresh water they should not drink sea water. While we need salt, the amount of salt in sea water would kill a person more quickly than thirst. Have a little too much salt on your popcorn and your kidneys will filter out the extra. But to do so, they need extra fresh water.

The marine iguanas of the Galapagos islands drink too much salt water every day. They feed on the algae that grow in sea water, but they lack a good freshwater supply to flush the salt out using their kidneys. Since God knew what kind of environment this iguana would one day be living in, He gave the marine iguana a special gland. Located in its head, it removes excess salt from the iguanas' blood and holds it. Periodically, the iguana will sneeze, expelling the salt-saturated fluid. As it dries it leaves a salty crown on the top of its head that dissolves back into the sea during the next swim. Several other reptiles also have salt glands, but each of these work very differently. This means that evolutionists must explain how these salt glands evolved at least ten times.

God gave the marine iguana these unique glands because He knew what they would need for the life He gave them.

Prayer: Thank You, Lord, for providing so wondrously for all Your creatures, even as you have provided for my salvation. Amen.

Ref: *Answers*, 3-4/09, pp. 20-22, Mary Mitchell, "Salt-Sneezing Lizards."

Star Smellers

Genesis 27:27a
"And he came near, and kissed him: and he smelled the smell of his raiment, and blessed him...."

Can mammals that spend time in the water smell odors under water? Of course they can, but no researcher is going to take a big sniff under water to find out!

Being able to smell helps us to learn important information about our surroundings – smells can attract or warn of danger. But it has always been thought that semi-aquatic animals could never smell odors under water. Animal researchers at Vanderbilt University were aware that water shrews and star-nosed moles release bubbles constantly when they are under water, but they didn't know why. The star-nosed mole is amazing by itself. Its nose has 16 pink tentacles, giving this strange-looking creature its name. So they watched the animals under water on high speed video. They saw the creatures exhaling and then re-inhaling the bubbles at the rate of ten times a second. That led them to wonder whether the animals could be detecting odors under water. As a test, they placed food in the tank but separated it from the test subjects with a screen so there was no physical contact. As the animals were tested they excitedly targeted in on the food source, demonstrating that they were indeed detecting the odor of wanted food.

Since these creatures make their living under water, God has given them the amazing and surprising ability to smell under water.

Prayer: Heavenly Father, the gifts You give are wonderful and often unexpected, for which I praise and thank You. Amen.

Ref: www.rscc.org/Chemistry World/News/2006/December/20120601.asp, "A breath of fresh water."

Hot Fungicide

Exodus 37:29

"And he made the holy anointing oil, and the pure incense of sweet spices, according to the work of the apothecary."

Plant seeds are distributed by a number of ingenious methods, including wind, water, mammals and birds. Plants that rely upon these creatures to distribute their seeds often attract them with tasty fruit surrounding the seed. However, tasty fruit contains sugar and other substances that many other creatures also find inviting. Yes, the problem is, everybody likes sugar and that includes insects, molds and fungi, all of which are useless as seed distributors. Some plants make up for this problem by producing large amounts of fruit, just to ensure that some are reproduced.

It has long been said that "hot" chili peppers use spice to deter non-seed distributors from contaminating their fruit. Researchers have now confirmed this and report that the "hot" taste in these chili peppers comes from the amount and types of chemicals in them called capsaicinoids. They studied the Capsicum chili plants in Bolivia that have a range of capsaicinoids. A common fruit pest in this part of the world is a sap-sucking bug whose mouth parts commonly infest plants with a black fungus. Researchers surveyed infestations in different plant populations and analyzed the quantity of capsaicinoids they contain. Sure enough, the hotter peppers had measurably fewer black mold infestations than the more mild peppers.

In providing these plants with protection from pests, God has also provided us with useful and pleasant spices.

Prayer: Father, thank You for not only providing protection for productive plants but for giving us useful spices as well. Amen.

Ref: www.sciencenews.org/view/generic/id/35114/title/Bittersweet_fruits, 8/12/08, Rachel Ehrenberg, "Bittersweet Fruits."

Capuchins Don't Monkey Around

Genesis 3:15

"And I will put enmity between thee and the woman, and between thy seed and her seed; it shall bruise thy head, and thou shalt bruise his heel."

We were once told that tool use is what separates man from the animals. Then it was discovered that some animals use tools. Now, scientists have learned that these animals do more than just grab something from their surroundings; they look for something that would be needed to do the job.

Primatologists studied tool use and selection among wild capuchin monkeys in Brazil. First, they observed natural tool use among the monkeys. They noticed that when monkeys wanted to crack open a nut they examined several types of stones. When they had a choice between a hard rock or a softer sandstone, which would be likely to break, they preferred the harder stone after examining both rocks. One monkey was observed examining two stones of the same hardness and then selecting the larger one. Then he placed a palm nut on a fallen log and cracked the nut open with a rock. Stone selection also varied depending on what type of nut was being cracked open.

Man isn't separated from animals by tool use or making. Rather, he is separated from animals because he was made to have a personal relationship with God. He is also responsible to God for his actions. This is why, when man first sinned, God promised us a Savior Who would show us the way to salvation.

Prayer: I thank You, Father, that through Your Son Jesus Christ I have the forgiveness of sins and salvation. Amen.

Ref: www.science news.org/view/generic/id/39930, 1/15/09, Bruce Bower, "Capuchin Monkeys Choose The Right Tool For The Nut."

Moths Fool Bats

2 Corinthians 11:14

"And no marvel; for Satan himself is transformed into an angel of light."

When one thinks of clever creatures, moths are probably not the first creature that come to mind – in fact, they probably don't come to mind at all!

Researchers at Wake Forest University raised some bats from infanthood in large cages. Their purpose was to carefully control the growing bats' diets and study their responses to various prey. Among the prey offered were Tiger moths. In the caterpillar stage they eat plants which make them unpalatable even as moths. As moths, when a bat is near, they emit a series of clicks. A bat will try to eat the moths only once, spitting out the foul-tasting insect almost immediately after biting it. When the bats were offered a different but equally foul-tasting species of Tiger moth, a few of the bats tried the new species despite their "don't eat me" clicking sounds. They quickly learned to avoid the new species as well. Researchers also offered the bats tasty Milkweed Tussock moths. While tasty, these moths click like the tiger moths when approached by a bat. Three of ten bats tried these moths, but the other seven wouldn't touch them. These tasty moths managed to fool most of the bats into thinking that they were the unpalatable Tiger moths.

Good doesn't usually mimic evil, but Scripture warns us that evil will mimic good.

Prayer: Father, thank You for Your Word which teaches me the truth of salvation and warns me against evil mimicking good. Amen.

Ref: *Science News*, 6/23/07, p. 397. S.M., "Moths mimic 'Don't eat me' sounds."

Man Is Not First to Do Genetic Engineering

Genesis 9:3

"Every moving thing that liveth shall be meat for you; even as the green herb have I given you all things."

"You are what you eat." We've all heard the saying. It doesn't mean that if you eat a lot of chicken, you'll literally become a chicken. But now science has discovered a creature for which the saying is literally true, in part, right down to the genetic level.

The green sea slug called *Elysia chlorotica* is more than just leaf-shaped. It eats algae and after a couple of weeks doesn't need to eat for the rest of its year-long life. It actually photosynthesizes its own food by stealing the genes for photosynthesis from the algae it ate. However, geneticists knew that the genetic information it steals from the algae only gives it one-tenth of the DNA it needs to code for the proteins needed to continue to be able to photosynthesize. In search of the answer to this mystery, scientists closely studied the slug's DNA. They discovered that the missing genetic information was indeed to be found in the slug. What's more, this information was identical to the algae's genetic information. In other words, the slug steals all of the genetic information necessary for photosynthesis. Scientists are mystified as to how the slug accomplishes this wonder!

Of course, it's no mystery when you know that the same Creator Who designed DNA also designed the sea slug who can selectively steal it.

Prayer: Father, I thank You for all the wonders You have created, but the greatest wonder is Your love toward me. Amen.

Ref: www.newscientist.com/article/dn16124-solarpowered-sea-slug-harnesses-stolen-plant-genes.html, 11/24/08, Catherine Brahic, "Solar-powered sea slug harnesses stolen plant genes."

Nasty Nannies

Romans 8:21

"Because the creature itself also shall be delivered from the bondage of corruption into the glorious liberty of the children of God."

There is a species of ant that, although quite small, makes slaves of yet smaller ants. This slave-making ant makes its nest inside acorns, and unlike the species they enslave, they have chemical weapons and powerful jaws.

While they enslave the smaller species, they don't seem to do much else, including caring for their own young. They get their captives by raiding the nests of the smaller species, stealing larvae and pupae. Once these ant babies mature in the acorn, they are expected to do all the work, including taking care of the slave-makers' eggs. Evolutionary scientists have said that such ants could not evolve resistance against their enslavement. However, now they have learned that the slave ants do indeed resist. Once the slave-maker's eggs mature to the pupa stage, the slave-ants will neglect them or even eat them. This is behavior they do not do in their home colony. Researchers say the slave-maker ant queens lay enough eggs. However, between 60 and 80 percent never make it to maturity when cared for by captive slaves. Such population reductions help reduce future raids on their home colonies – home colonies they have never seen! Clearly, an altruistic objective.

But not all slavery is physical. God sent His Son, Jesus Christ, to be our Lord and Savior when we were enslaved by sin, death and the devil.

Prayer: Thank You, Father, for sending Your Son, Jesus Christ, to free me from bondage to sin, death and the devil. Amen.

Ref: www.sciencenews.org/view/generic/id/35309/title/Slave_ants-rebel, Susan Milius, "Slave Ants Rebel."

Birds' Unique Leg Structure Says No Evolution

Genesis 1:21

"And God created ... every winged fowl after his kind: and God saw that it was good."

Countless television programs, museums, textbooks, and popular articles tell us that the birds evolved from dinosaurs. It now appears that this claim is even *less* credible!

Researchers at Oregon State University have made a fundamental discovery about how birds breathe. Unlike other land animals, birds have immovable thigh bones, and they walk and run by bending their knees. All other land creatures can move both their thigh bone as well as bend their knees to walk and run. This included the dinosaurs and other theropods from which birds supposedly evolved. Birds need twenty times as much oxygen as cold-blooded animals. To supply this need, birds are designed with unique lungs and supporting musculature. Researchers found that if birds had the usual muscle structures and could move their thighs, their high-performance lungs would collapse. Even the evolutionists at Oregon State University said that this makes it unlikely that birds evolved from dinosaurs, and they added that birds appear earlier in the fossil record than the theropods from which they supposedly evolved!

There are other transition problems associated with bird evolution that are seldom mentioned. For example, reptiles are cold-blooded and birds are warm blooded; yet, this major transition has seemingly been overlooked.

Of course, the Bible has always taught that birds were specially made by God and did not evolve from any other creature.

Prayer: Lord, You have designed all things well. Do not let Your people be fooled by those who deny Your works. Amen.

Ref: Oregon State University (2009, June 9), "Discovery Raises New Doubts About Dinosaur -Bird Links. *Science Daily*. Retrieved June 16, 2009, from http://www.sciencedaily.com/ releases/2009/06/090609092055.htm.

Monkeying with Genetics

Psalm 7:17

"What is man, that thou shouldest magnify him? and that thou shouldest set thine heart upon him?"

We have all heard the claims – and school textbooks love to include it – that humans and chimpanzees are about 99 percent genetically identical. However, that claim evaporates when the details of what is being compared are examined.

First of all, the DNA sequences that were compared were cherry-picked. Similar sequences in both humans and chimps were compared, while non-similar sequences were ignored. In addition, comparisons were made using only the DNA that codes for making protein. This ignores most of the human and chimp genome. When the DNA that regulates cell operation are included in the comparison, the degree of similarity drops considerably. Important parts of certain chromosomes, like the Y chromosome, are very different. Research has also found that there are major differences between how certain genes express themselves within cells. In addition, the chimpanzee genome is 10 to 12 percent larger than man's, which is quite a difference in itself.

The truth is the entire human and chimp genome has never been properly compared, while if it has, it has never been reported. However, when the spiritual differences are considered, there is an unbridgeable gulf between humans and chimps. Man was made in the image of God, to be responsible before Him and to have a relationship with Him. Jesus Christ died for the salvation of mankind, not for chimps.

Prayer: Thank You, Father, for sending Your Son for our redemption and seeking us out with Your gracious Word. Amen.

Ref: *Acts & Facts*, 6/09, pp. 12-13, Jeffery Tomkins, Human-Chimp Similarities, "Common Ancestry or Flawed Research?"

New Avian Speed Champion Discovered

Job 9:10

"Which doeth great things past finding out; yea, and wonders without number."

A peregrine falcon diving toward its prey reaches a relative speed of 200 body-lengths per second. This is close to the 207 body-lengths that the space shuttle travels as it enters our atmosphere. Thus, the peregrine falcon was thought to easily be the fastest dare-devil bird on Earth.

Scientists have now discovered that a little pink male hummingbird called Anna's Hummingbird is the real Top Gun among the birds. As part of its mating ritual, a male hummingbird will try to impress a female with his speed and acrobatics. First, the male will fly up to about 90 feet above the ground. Then, he begins a power dive. As he nears the female, he pulls up, ascending again. During that near-miss pull-up he experiences more than nine times the force of gravity. His relative speed during descent is 385 body-lengths per second. That's almost twice the peregrine falcon's relative speed, it's faster than the space shuttle entering the Earth's atmosphere and is more than twice the relative speed of a jet fighter running with afterburners!

The wonders of God's creation are still being discovered, and Creation Moments still loves to make them known to our listeners. But God's greatest wonder is His love for us though His Son, Jesus Christ. We are thankful that this wonder is revealed to us in the Bible.

Prayer: Father, I give You thanks for the wonders You create, but I especially give You thanks for the wonder of salvation. Amen.

Ref: *Science News*, 7/4/09, p. 7, Susan Millius, "Hummingbird pulls Top Gun stunts."

Worm's Glue May Fix You

Job 12:7

"But ask now the beasts, and they shall teach thee; and the fowls of the air, and they shall tell thee...."

While materials scientists are always interested in super-strong glues, they are especially interested in super-strong glues that harden under water. It turns out that a small marine worm called the Sandcastle Worm has a few things to teach them.

The Sandcastle Worm builds itself a tube-like shell by gluing together sand particles and bits of shell. It is the glue it uses that is of interest to scientists. This amazing glue not only hardens under water, it hardens in 30 seconds. The glue comes from a special gland in the Sandcastle Worm. While it hardens quickly, after several hours it becomes like leather. After analyzing it, scientists identified several of the proteins that are responsible for its properties. They also found that half those proteins are either very negatively or very positively charged. Attempting to mimic the glue, scientists mixed together some of the same charged proteins to see if they would bond broken bone together in a wet environment. Their glue not only bonded the bone together, but remained neither acid nor alkaline which is crucial for materials used in living bodies. Scientists also report that the glue is not poisonous.

As we study how God created things, we are learning better ways to do things. This is surely evidence that an intelligent Creator is responsible for the creation.

Prayer: Father, prosper all good learning and knowledge, and keep us from falling into false knowledge. Amen.

Ref: Science News Online, http://www.sciencenews.org/index/activity/view/id/46544/title/worm-inspired_superglue, Rachel Ehrenbergm, "Worm-Inspired Superglue."

Magpies Reflect on Themselves

2 Chronicles 9:23

"And all the kings of the earth sought the presence of Solomon, to hear his wisdom, that God had put in his heart."

When you look in a mirror you are conscious of seeing yourself. Bottlenose dolphins, elephants and primates in general have also shown this ability, but that's about it.

Since social birds, like magpies, have larger brains than other birds, researchers wanted to find out if they would recognize themselves in a mirror. To do this, researchers placed a mark on the animal that can only be seen or touched when they look into the mirror. Most animals would have no idea that the creature in the mirror was themselves. Many animals would simply look behind the mirror and be puzzled. Even if they didn't, their lack of recognition of themselves would become evident when they did *not* seek to remove the unnatural spot from the image in the mirror. Researchers found that most magpies recognized the image in a mirror as themselves and sought to remove the unnatural mark from their own body while looking in the mirror. When given a choice, most of the magpies also preferred the compartment with a mirror in a two-compartment cage. The minority of magpies that didn't recognize themselves in the mirror preferred the compartment without a mirror.

It should be clear that attributes such as consciousness, wisdom and knowledge cannot be created by accident and chance. Only God could grant these things as His creatures need them.

Prayer: Father, I thank You for the gifts of wisdom and knowledge. Help me to use these gifts to Your glory. Amen.

Ref: http://www.sciencenews.org/view/generic/id/35462/title/1%2_magpie, Bruce Bower, "I Magpie."

Killer Plants

Genesis 3:18

"Thorns also and thistles shall it bring forth to thee; and thou shalt eat the herb of the field;"

Ever since sin came into the world, unwanted plants have stolen from the productivity of man's food crops. Man has concocted some herbicides to help control weeds, but these can have some unwanted effects as well.

Scientists are now learning from the plants themselves. They have discovered that many plants make their own herbicides to keep competing species from taking their water and nutrients. Many of these herbicides are potent and plant specific. For example, certain types of fine fescue grasses secrete a modified form of tyrosine. Twenty of the most common urban weeds absorb the modified form of tyrosine as if it were the real, nutritious form and soon stunt and die. The fescue produces a lush, slow growing lawn. The crop plant sorghum has been found to produce a slow release herbicide. Selective breeding has been used to increase this characteristic and test crops are planned. Mustards, cabbages and broccoli also produce their own herbicide, and as a bonus, they fix nitrogen in the soil. Studies are underway to learn whether they could be rotated with other crops for both weed control and fertilization.

While man's sin has subjected the creation to futility, God has given His creation the ability to still be productive. Thankfully, He has given us an eternal solution to sin, as well.

Prayer: Father, I thank You that you have provided us with a solution to our sin in the hope we have now and eternal life. Amen.

Ref: *Science News*, 3/17/07, pp. 167-169, Janet Raloff, "Herbal Herbicide."

The Biggest Chicken You Never Saw?

Genesis 1:24

"And God said, Let the earth bring forth the living creature after his kind, cattle, and creeping thing, and beast of the earth after his kind: and it was so."

In a previous *Creation Moments* we reported on the finding of unfossilized soft tissue in a *T. Rex* fossil. Subsequent study of the soft tissue revealed collagen which has identifiable DNA. Even many evolutionary scientists have admitted that this fact calls into question the claim that dinosaurs died out 65 million years ago.

As a result of the DNA studies of this dinosaur collagen, a recent study cautiously announced the conclusion that the closest match to the *T. Rex* DNA was chicken DNA. This was taken much less cautiously by the media as proof that birds evolved from dinosaurs. In fact, the similarity between the *T. Rex* DNA and chicken DNA was only 58 percent. For comparison, the similarity between human DNA and frog DNA is 81 percent. The similarity of human DNA and cow DNA is 97 percent. Some segments of the *T. Rex* DNA matched mice, frogs and even fish. The original authors of the study also pointed out that the DNA database they used is not complete. It is entirely likely that a better match than only 58 percent would have been found if the database had contained more animals.

The lesson here is that the popular media is often much less cautious about so-called evolutionary proofs than are the professional scientists.

Prayer: I thank You, Father, for the beautiful variety of creatures You have created. Let me not be misled by the world. Amen.

Ref: www.answersingenesis.org/articles/2007/04/13/t-rex-big-chicken

Jays Anticipate, Prevent Theft

Matthew 6:20

"But lay up for yourselves treasures in heaven, where neither moth nor rust doth corrupt, and where thieves do not break through nor steal."

People are aware that others could steal from them. That's why we put locks on our doors and lock our cars. Sometimes we even hide things that might be stolen.

While they don't use locks, it turns out that western scrub jays do hide food anticipating that it might be stolen. In the lab, scrub jays typically cache uneaten food in ice cube trays filled with pellets. The jays have a hierarchy, with higher and lower ranked birds. Lower ranked birds do not steal food from higher ranked birds, but they will steal from their peers. When a lone jay was given a favorite food, he hid it with apparent randomness. There was a similar pattern when a bird of lower status was watching. However, when a bird of equal or greater status was watching, the caching jay would return and move his treats once the jay who was watching left. If they had a choice, they would hide their mealworms further from the watcher. Researchers noted that this behavior reveals two unexpected results. Not only can the jays tell the difference between individuals, they can anticipate theft.

Researchers found the jays' abilities quite, as one of them put it, "impressive," given that their brains are much less evolved than ours. Of course, they were actually given these abilities by their Creator.

Prayer: Father, help me to value those things You provide that are heavenly and let not earthly things distract me. Amen.

Ref: *Science News*, 5/20/06, p. 309, S. Milius, "Jay Watch."

Humming Bats

Psalm 119:103

"How sweet are thy words unto my taste! yea, sweeter than honey to my mouth!"

Hummingbirds have to have a very special metabolism because they are such tiny, warm-blooded creatures and they must move their wings furiously. Unlike other animals, hummingbirds don't store the sugars they eat for later use. They metabolize them immediately.

Scientists were studying the unique South American long-tongued bat. These unusual mammals hover at flowers like hummingbirds and feed on the nectar. Scientists got to wondering how they generated the high amount of energy they need from the sugars in the nectar. Nectar usually contains several different kinds of sugars. They kept their experimental long-tongued bats on a nectar diet with its multiple sugar formula. Then they changed the bats' diet to one of three sugars, glucose, fructose or sucrose. By monitoring their breath, scientists could tell how quickly the bats began metabolizing their new diet. Scientists report that the bats began metabolizing the new diet within minutes of receiving it. No other mammal, no other creature, except the hummingbird, is able to do this.

It would be difficult to explain how such a unique ability could evolve twice is such different creatures. But we could say that God just wanted to make a mammal with the characteristics of a hummingbird to show that such creatures don't happen by accident.

Prayer: Lord, feed me with Your Word that I may know its sweetness and grow in faith. Amen.

Ref: *Science News*, 9/1/07, p. 141, C. B., "Bats Hum for Sugar Too."

Honeybees Won't Be Fooled on Colors

Isaiah 54:11

"O thou afflicted, tossed with tempest, and not comforted, behold, I will lay thy stones with fair colours, and lay thy foundations with sapphires."

If you've ever mixed up some navy blue socks with some black socks because the light wasn't bright enough you know that lighting is crucial for determining colors. Different lighting and different hues of colored light can easily fool a person.

Researchers at University College London wanted to know if different hues of light would fool honeybees. After all, fine distinction of color is important for their survival. They already knew that bees can see color. First, they set up an arrangement of different colored fake flowers, only one of which consistently provided them a reward. As they rearranged the flowers, the same color always gave the reward. This trained the bees to seek out that color flower. Then they tested whether the bees could find their moving target as they were lit with different hues of light. They found that the bees were never fooled by the different lighting. They always went right to the target flower. This demonstrated that honeybees have a much greater ability to process color information under differing conditions than suspected.

Color is definitely a gift of God. As He speaks in picture language about the New Testament church through Isaiah, God describes its beauty in terms of fair colors, among other things. God knew that color recognition is crucial to the survival of honeybees.

Prayer: Thank You, Lord, for using Your gift of color so extravagantly in the creation. Amen.

Ref: *Photonics Spectra*, 12/05, p. 172, "Beeline for Color."

Letting God Create Your Day, Volume 7 Index